TAKE ME OUTSIDE

TAKE ME OUTSIDE

Running Across the
Canadian Landscape
That Shapes Us

COLIN HARRIS

RMB

Copyright © 2021 by Colin Harris
First Edition

For information on purchasing bulk quantities of this book, or to obtain media excerpts or invite the author to speak at an event, please visit rmbooks.com and select the "Contact" tab.

RMB | Rocky Mountain Books Ltd.
rmbooks.com
@rmbooks
facebook.com/rmbooks

Cataloguing data available from Library and Archives Canada

ISBN 9781771604659 (softcover)
ISBN 9781771604666 (electronic)

Cover design by Lyuba Kirkova
Printed and bound in Canada

We would like to also take this opportunity to acknowledge the traditional territories upon which we live and work. In Calgary, Alberta, we acknowledge the Niitsítapi (Blackfoot) and the people of the Treaty 7 region in Southern Alberta, which includes the Siksika, the Piikuni, the Kainai, the Tsuut'ina, and the Stoney Nakoda First Nations, including Chiniki, Bearpaw, and Wesley First Nations. The City of Calgary is also home to Métis Nation of Alberta, Region III. In Victoria, British Columbia, we acknowledge the traditional territories of the Lkwungen (Esquimalt and Songhees), Malahat, Pacheedaht, Scia'new, T'Sou-ke, and W̱SÁNEĆ (Pauquachin, Tsartlip, Tsawout, Tseycum) peoples.

We acknowledge the financial support of the Government of Canada through the Canada Book Fund and the Canada Council for the Arts, and of the province of British Columbia through the British Columbia Arts Council and the Book Publishing Tax Credit.

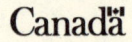

For my parents, Ray and Cathie Harris

CONTENTS

Prologue	9
Chapter 1: Growing Convictions	13
Chapter 2: Winter on "The Rock"	33
Chapter 3: Learning Outside	59
Chapter 4: Spring Awakening	77
Chapter 5: A Hard Goodbye	101
Chapter 6: Alone	121
Chapter 7: Like Father, Like Son	143
Chapter 8: Prairie Skies	165
Chapter 9: Homestretch	185
Chapter 10: The End and the Beginning	203
Epilogue	225
Acknowledgements	233
Selected Sources	237
About the Author	239

PROLOGUE

> When you think about Canadians, you might ask yourself: Why are we the way we are? Well the answer is lying right under our feet, literally. Fact is, it's this land that shapes us. There's a reason why we run off the dock instead of tippy-toe in. It's because that water is frozen six months a year. And that frozen water brought on a sport that we can call our own. This land is unlike any other. We have more square feet of awesomeness per person than any other nation on Earth. It's why we flock towards lakes, mountains, forests, rivers and streams. We know we have the best backyard in the world. And we get out there every chance we get. Because it's not just the great outdoors we're chasing, it's freedom. And this place gives it to us at every turn. Here, we're free to chill out, unwind and free to wind up.
>
> —Molson Canadian beer commercial, YouTube, 2010

For many, there's a sense of pride in being called Canadian. For others, it's a label that doesn't resonate; it's become tainted or even rejected. There are numerous issues that divide us and make us different from one another, be it politics, socio-economic status, cultural background or even gender. So it seems rather naive to think that anyone, including a beer company's advertising for the 2010 Winter Olympics in Vancouver, can encapsulate what it means to be a Canadian in a few phrases. But what unites us? What binds all of us who live in this country together? Exploring what it means to be Canadian helps to tell the story of this country. It is these stories that help shape our history and culture, or rather histories and cultures. As this country is discovering, some of these stories aren't easy to tell. They involve pain, misgivings and decisions that have proved harmful. But working through these stories can help make our collective identity as a diverse country stronger.

The common ground that connects us all is this land we're so fortunate to live on. Our geography shapes us, not only as human beings but also as a nation. Our identity as Canadians is rooted in our relationship with the land and the time we spend outside. But, increasingly, it seems as though this relationship might be in jeopardy. We are no longer getting "out there every chance we get." Our relationship with the outdoors has shifted. We seem more disconnected, retreating into an interior world of streaming, gaming, scrolling and shopping – it's all too easy. A recent study showed that 74 per cent of Canadian adults would rather stay inside than head outdoors, even though 87 per cent know that going outside is good for them. Should we just accept this new reality? Are we even conscious of this shift? Is it making us less Canadian? And it's not just adults who are spending less time outside; younger generations are too, and it's a cause for concern. So why aren't we spending as much time outside anymore?

My desire to engage young Canadians in this conversation about our shift away from nature and spending time outside manifested in a combination of two goals: a dream to run across the country and a desire to launch a nonprofit organization to help contribute to the conversation. The seed for running across Canada was planted when I was a young teenager. It grew slowly but steadily, weaving its way in and out of my consciousness for years. Starting a nonprofit was a more recent goal, but I wanted this journey to have a sense of purpose, which I found not only through my work as an outdoor and environmental educator but also through my collective experiences throughout childhood. I was ill-equipped for either goal – but my convictions were sound and irrefutable. My commitment to this was unwavering, although I had yet to tell my parents. For good reason, I procrastinated in sharing my latest vision with my mother and father. The number of times I approached them with various life plans and half-baked ideas were too many to count. When I was 14 years old, I professed my desire to be a professional baseball player.

"But you don't currently play baseball, Colin," my mom said, flatly.

After the 2000 Summer Olympics in Sydney, Australia, I proclaimed I would be heading to a future Olympics.

"For what sport?" my dad asked.

"Marathon or table tennis," I replied, although I had never run a full marathon and my trophies from junior high Ping-Pong were collecting dust in a box.

A year before I was to begin my journey across Canada, I asked my parents to join me at their dining room table when I was home for Christmas. I had a new plan.

"What would you say if I told you I was thinking about running across Canada?"

CHAPTER 1

Growing Convictions

> How we spend our days is, of course,
> how we spend our lives.
> —Annie Dillard

Perhaps embarking on a journey begins first from a meaningful story. Whether it's an accumulation of experiences or a collection of beliefs, the story helps shape the journey's course, causing it to evolve into something more substantive. Our convictions matter. At least that's what my father instilled in me. My convictions became a journey of their own, carving their way through the Canadian landscapes I grew up in.

I was too young to remember the harsh winter winds that blow through the Red Deer River Valley 150 kilometres east of the Rocky Mountains. I can't recall the thin spires of rock rising from the flat, grassy fields that continue to reveal buried remains of prehistoric creatures. Yet I'm certain this landscape started shaping me from my first breaths.

As I was the first-born in my family, my mother was inundated with unsolicited advice on how to raise a well-rounded child, despite her degree in nursing. In those first weeks of my life, amid the fog of sleepless nights and countless diaper changes, the advice she took to heart came from an opinionated accountant with jet-black hair who lived in the house beside my parents.

"Take him outside every day, so he gets used to the cold," she offered, unapologetically.

It wasn't bad advice for being born in Drumheller in mid-December. However, those daily outings in the heart of the Alberta badlands required time, effort and commitment from my mother and, to this day, she continues to take credit for acclimatizing me to the cold, harsh prairie winters, of which I would experience many.

As our family moved from city to city over the years due to my parents' shared vocation, my childhood was unknowingly impacted by the time I spent outside. In those early years, it was my parents' dedication to daily outdoor time that presumably formed the basis of my convictions to come decades later. My father, not knowing what else to do with me while tending to laundry, would put me in a clothesbasket on the porch as he hung bedsheets and sweatshirts to dry in the backyard. On one such occasion, he discovered that a 6-month-old has the dexterity and determination to roll a flimsy piece of plastic on its side. He found me at the bottom of the porch, still intact. At family dinners it too is something he continues to take credit for, always with a sly smile.

I became a brother when we moved southwest to the

foothills of the Rocky Mountains. Calgary is where I discovered my love for playgrounds. I built sandcastles, slid down long and shiny strips of metal and yelled, "Higher!" as my mom pushed my sister Kristen and me on the swings. I learned how to throw rocks into the Bow River and mold the mud from its banks in the palms of my hands. My mother promises we were taken to the mountains on occasion, but I have no early memories of those dramatic peaks.

I was too young to have any real awareness of the oil sands or the surrounding boreal forest and rivers as we moved north to Fort McMurray, where I again became a brother to my youngest sister, Alison. Rather, I had an obsession with playing marbles in the backyard, running away and hiding after ringing neighbours' doorbells, and learning to ride a bike.

When my family moved to the peninsula of land north of Lake Ontario, the main gathering space for my friends and me became the yard outside of our apartment building in Toronto. There was a fenced-in playground with swings and monkey bars, but it was a maple tree standing tall just beyond the enclosed playground that captured our attention. We scrambled high and swung from its branches, but more often than not the extended arms of the maple offered an invitation to simply sit. It was there we solved the problems of the world, or at least those deemed important by 10-year-olds.

It was our move a few years later to the eastern edge

of the prairies, into the Red River Valley, that opened the floodgates for me. Snowdrifts taller than my father were perfect for digging snow tunnels at the side of our house in Winnipeg. When it wasn't winter, quiet alleyways were conducive to bike rides and hushed conversations among friends. My family lived across from a small park where activities ranged from box baseball to bantering bullies – I excelled at the former and was a target for the latter. Further down from the small park were Sturgeon Creek and wide open spaces that were once covered in tall prairie grass. Every kid I knew, including me, seemed to have an expansive radius from home to roam, explore and play. In today's vernacular, we were all free-range kids. It wasn't a conscious choice by our parents; it's just how it was.

In 1988, as I was navigating junior high in Winnipeg, Calgary hosted the Winter Olympics. The Olympic torch relay was making its way westward across Canada before the start of the Games, and our school, Ness Junior High, was let out at midday to watch the torchbearer run along historic Portage Avenue. We all had miniature Petro-Canada torches in hand, eager to have them lit by the official torch. Portage Avenue was more electric than I was accustomed to. My friends and I stood outside of Hilmar Venture, one of the world's greatest candy stores (that also happened to make trophies), eagerly awaiting the first glance at the Olympic flame. Security measures were either carefully hidden or simply nonexistent, so as the torch passed in front of me, I began to run with the small entourage surrounding the torchbearer, as did many of my classmates.

For most, the anticipation of having their miniature torches lit fizzled out rather quickly. After a couple of hundred metres, coldness and boredom set in simultaneously, and my classmates veered off to walk back to school. However, my legs kept running. Fuelled by the crisp December air, a blue prairie sky and the sugar rush of ten-cent candies, I ran quietly beside the torch, unaware of the diminishing crowds as we approached the city limits. I wanted to keep running, but at the overpass that marked the perimeter highway and the western edge of the city, the torchbearer hopped into the back of the support vehicle. Within moments, the flashing lights faded and I stood alone on the shoulder of the Trans-Canada Highway. The walk back to school felt long, but as time passed, a seed was planted. That winter, I watched athletes on TV like Michael Edwards, better known as Eddie the Eagle, Britain's failed but beloved ski jumper who won the hearts of people around the world. I was drawn in by his story and his dream and realized I wanted to create a dream of my own.

After I'd built some solid friendships and a sense of belonging during my years in the prairie capital, our family was unexpectedly relocated from Winnipeg back to Toronto. I had lived in Toronto years before, but moving this time was considerably more difficult. Leaving good friends behind and foraging for new ones at the beginning of my high school career seemed a daunting task. Another family who worked for the same organization as my parents lived five doors down from the house we moved into and they too had a son my age. Our mothers conspired, as I needed some friends, and Dave needed some *new* friends – the crowd he was hanging out with found trouble on a daily basis, the kind of trouble that keeps parents waiting for the phone to ring at night. On a humid July afternoon, there was a knock on the door and my mother called me up from the basement. I'm sure there were similarities between this grunge rock fan and me, but first encounters leave an impression and I couldn't hide my look of disdain. Dave wore cut-off jean shorts and purple Doc Martens, and his gelled hair added the length of a choice finger to his height. Who was this skateboarding punk at my front door? Our mothers introduced us and a forced "hello" was uttered, but our moms carried the conversation from there. It was awkward and embarrassing, not to mention a waste of time. I was sure I would never become friends with him.

My mother relentlessly pursued her hidden agenda, telling me I should call Dave and do something with him. *I'd rather do anything than something with him*, I thought. But I could only ward her off for so long – my mother has a knack for persuasion. Within a week of our introduction on the front porch, I begrudgingly called Dave and asked him if he wanted to go for a bike ride. He agreed, likely because of his own mother's convincing ways. I rode over to his place and we headed down into Sunnybrook Park, which dipped into a valley behind our neighbourhood.

"So, do you like sports?" I asked quietly, as we started riding.

"Nope, not really," he replied.

For the next 45 minutes, we rode in silence. Not another word was spoken, only the chains on our bikes saved us from the roaring silence. As we made our way through the park, tree branches swayed quietly in the wind. The Don River was not in good shape, pollution had taken its toll, but the current was mesmerizing as it wrapped around rocks and over ledges. Birds made their nests above, and dogs fetched sticks in the lush grass. Alice Kilgour gifted this 175-acre property to the citizens of Toronto in 1928 in memory of her late husband Joseph, and it would become a place where children played daily and made new discoveries. The serenity of that park would prove monumental in the years to come, but in that uncomfortable moment, Dave and I were lost for words. We didn't speak again that summer.

Over the course of the next year, our friendship slowly found its way. Due to the fact of being neighbours and our parents' similar work, our families saw each other numerous times a week. A strong bond began to grow as the seasonal cycle of birth and death repeated itself each spring and fall. It was a friendship that would see the purchase of our first vehicle, a 1970 Volkswagen camper van we named Finnegan that spent more time in the shop and the driveway than it did on the open road. It was a friendship that would see cancer consume Dave's father in the upstairs bedroom of their family home. It was a friendship that would see road trips and canoe trips, more bike rides and even the occasional run in Sunnybrook Park. It turned out Dave was more outdoorsy than he let on. However, countless evenings were simply spent sitting on the curb outside his house, spitting puddles onto the cement between our legs as we talked about music, relationships and the hardships of being a teenager. It was here where, among many stories shared, I voiced my dream of running across Canada. Dave was the first person I told.

In the years to come, my experiences outside would not only mold me, they would begin to direct the path I would travel. My uncle's family owned a small, rustic cabin north of Toronto with a composting toilet and a clear set of rules for its use tacked to the adjacent wall. The cabin was on a relatively small lake, and so on one summer visit, I felt compelled to take the canoe out on my own. I had paddled before with a partner but never alone. As I headed south, the lack of a partner to share the paddling with wasn't a concern. I had read stories and watched movies and documentaries that all involved the canoe. At the time, this seemed a rite of passage to my identity: I was proud to be Canadian, and I revelled in every stroke I took to the end of the lake.

That pride quickly vanished as I turned the canoe north to head back. Paddling against the wind, a wind I did not notice on the way out, was an obstacle I had not expected nor was prepared for. The bow of the canoe was at the mercy of the wind as I fought to keep a straight line. I had no semblance of a J-stroke, my skill was limited to paddling as hard as I could. Even with all the strength my puberty-stricken body could muster, the wind had full control. After several minutes of getting nowhere, both the canoe and I were relegated to the rocky shore. I clambered out, knee deep with my running shoes on, and slowly started to wade back along the shoreline toward my uncle's property. Feeling defeated and humiliated, I kept my head down as I passed other cottages, residents smiling wryly behind their pickled Caesars and cedar decks. Although I felt defeated in that moment, it would not deter me from my growing admiration for this beloved form of Canadian travel.

I had settled into life in Toronto, but my runs through Sunnybrook Park, with or without Dave, were inconsistent at best. I dragged my feet through high school and then dragged them some more through university. After four years of studying music at the University of Toronto, I craved something different – a change from the black and white of reading music, looking at fractioned notes on pieces of paper. There was a job fair on campus promising employment for the coming summer, and a company hiring tree planters caught my attention. I was hired on the spot despite my complete lack of experience. In early May, I reported to an open patch of field outside of Chapleau in Northern Ontario.

I didn't know anyone, and although comfortable among friends, I was painfully shy and introverted with others. But spending every day outside evoked my romantic vision of long hard days connecting to the land while fighting black flies, mosquitoes and maybe even the odd black bear.

Romance trumped reality in those first couple of days of toiling to exhaustion and collapsing in my small tent, surrounded by 40 others in an uninspiring, nondescript field. However, reality would soon appear as I calculated my earnings from my first couple of days. I had not been briefed on the financial bottom line of tree planting as a rookie. By the third day, I was close to my tipping point, wondering if this was viable. With meticulous effort, I had planted my allotment of seedlings into the scarred land. Despite apparently delusional confidence in my technique, dozens of trees were flagged for subpar planting. After ten hours of work, I had successfully planted enough trees to earn $16. Camp costs were $25 a day – which included some of the best meals I've ever eaten – but even for someone who struggled through math class, the numbers did not add up. At the end of the day, I found my supervisor shovelling down his dinner in a nearby trailer, and, staring at my dusty work boots, I humbly presented an excuse of a family issue back home. Relief washed over my tired body as I drove south toward civilization. However, not long after my departure from the wilds of Northern Ontario, regret would find me. I yearned to dirty my hands and feel the warmth of the sun on my skin, regardless of the pay.

I ended up in Parry Sound that summer, sheepishly serving fresh fish and expensive wine to Toronto's cottage country. I rented a garden shed complete with a thin mattress on top of a plank of wood and a posse of scurrying mice. Every free moment outside of the restaurant was spent exploring the waters of Georgian Bay. I learned to fish and navigate rocky shorelines by kayak. I soared off cliffs caught by cool, pristine water and breathed in remarkable sunsets night after night, my love for the Canadian Shield deepening with each adventure. Afternoon runs along dirt roads were plentiful, and as my legs pounded out a steady pace, I often revisited that cross-Canada dream, wondering what it would take to run from the Atlantic Ocean to the Pacific.

As summers in Canada tend to unfold, it was over just as it was getting started. On a whim, I applied for a volunteer opportunity in Fort Smith, just across the Alberta border in the Northwest Territories. Having never been to the North before, I was awestruck as the plane landed in the tiny airport some 1100 kilometres north of Edmonton. The landscape was barren yet magical. The Slave River was mighty yet serene. My supervisor collected me from the airport and delivered me to a small campus where I would spend the next five months, working with Indigenous students from small settlements throughout the territory. The high school–aged teens were partaking in a leadership program aimed at attaining high enough marks to earn a post-secondary opportunity. My job was a cross between a live-in tutor, chef and counsellor. The leadership program filled my evenings and weekends, so I was able to add some daytime work as a substitute teacher at the local elementary school. Weekends were spent camping with the leadership students and connecting with the land. I became the student in those moments, learning Traditional Knowledge passed down through the generations of Indigenous people who had inhabited the land for centuries.

One evening in late September, after darkness had settled in, the students at the residency called me outside. I walked through the front doors into the cool night.

"Look up," they said in unison.

When I did, I couldn't comprehend what was happening. For a moment, I thought the students were projecting a laser show onto the starry night sky, but it was the aurora borealis like I had never seen it before. The northern lights were so low in the sky it felt as though I could extend my arm and touch the gloriously dancing hues of reds, blues, purples and greens. Its energy was overwhelming. In the five months I lived in Fort Smith, I was fortunate to see the northern lights many times, but never again as powerful, close and colourful as that first night.

In time, I found a partner to join me on harsh winter days running the long open expanses of small highways with little traffic. Laurie Dexter had one of the worst running forms I had ever seen. Hunched over, with short powerful tree trunks as legs, he quickly proved his endurance and stamina. I learned that Laurie had skied for 91 days from Russia to Canada via the North Pole. He had also skied to the South Pole, run 600 kilometres in six days, made numerous first ascents in the Arctic and had been to Antarctica more than 90 times. For his efforts and the work he did in the North, he received the Order of Canada. My recollection of those conversations while trying to keep up are few, but his inaudible perseverance was an example of human possibility, a sense of hope for this dream of running across the country that continued to have a grasp on me. Amid all these accolades, I simply remember him telling me to shorten my stride.

By February, I was back in Toronto, living in my parents' basement and working at a running store. It didn't take long for the restlessness to set in. By spring, I was applying for summer jobs, and at the top of the list was a desire to be a canoe tripper. Ontario camps were hiring and, before long, I was sitting in a living room in Toronto, chatting with Margaret and Marcello, the owners of a Lake Temagami–based camp. Over the course of an hour, they never once asked about my canoeing skills. I was thankful since my most recent experience was the failed attempt at my uncle's cottage. In mid-May, I boarded a school bus full of staff, most of whom were several years younger than me, and we drove toward Temagami, with its interconnected lake systems and rugged Canadian Shield, hours north of Toronto. Had the bus not pulled right up to a dock, our gear tossed directly onto a boat and immediately shipped off to an island, I would have surely bailed. This time, I was stuck. My introverted tendencies would have to find a way to cope.

The first canoe trip I led that summer was a four-day venture through the waters of Temagami with a group of 12-year-old boys and their two counsellors. As we paddled eastward away from camp, I felt a twinge of excitement: *I'm actually doing this. No one knows about my paddling skills, or lack thereof.* About 20 minutes into our trip, Marcello pulled up beside our canoes in the rather sizeable camp motorboat.

"Did you forget anything, Colin?"

"I don't think so," I replied, scouring my brain for the meaning behind his line of questioning.

A camper slowly emerged on the deck beside Marcello as he pulled him up by his lifejacket.

"You forgot a camper," he said sternly, his stare boring into me.

I didn't know what to say. I was embarrassed and dumbfounded. To be fair, the camper's actual counsellors hadn't noticed either, but the blame seemed to lie squarely on my shoulders, according to the direction of his stare. Marcello uttered some reassuring words that were directed more at the kids in the canoes than at me and then motored away leaving a wake of remorse. I laughed it off and the incident was soon washed away in the cleansing waters of Lake Temagami. We arrived at our destination later that afternoon and chores were delegated to establish camp. Firewood was to be collected, vegetables chopped for dinner and tents needed to be pitched.

"Where are the tents?" a counsellor inquired.

A flurry of activity followed as I ripped through the canoes. My second mistake of the day felt more reprehensible: I had forgotten all the tents in the tripper cabin, a five-hour paddle away. Panic set in as I realized the only solution to this situation involved paddling to a cottage I had spotted on a nearby island, hoping there was a phone and calling back to camp, more precisely, calling Marcello. I cringed as I waited on the phone for someone to find him. How could I have messed up so badly? Would I be fired before my first trip was even under my belt? He listened as I explained what happened.

"Start paddling back the way you came."

"Yes sir," I replied.

Thanks to horsepower more formidable than our paddles, we had our tents within an hour. We arrived back to camp four days later, boys happy, well fed and tired. The rest of my trips that summer went without incident, but I was elbowed and ribbed daily as a reminder of that first adventure, always with a smile.

Spending my working hours outside rather than sitting at a desk for eight hours appealed to me. After a summer leading canoe trips, I devised a plan to spend even more time outdoors braving the elements instead of staring at a computer screen. That fall, I was introduced to an outdoor education centre in Haliburton, one of the higher points of the Canadian Shield in central Ontario. Students from cities mostly to the south would venture north for three to five days, stay in cabins, eat at long communal tables and learn outdoor skills like how to paddle a canoe, use a map and compass and build a proper fire. And I got to teach these students how to do it.

It was a dream job. I would often pause in the middle of a canoe lesson, watching students practise their draws and pries against the backdrop of red and orange maples that lined the shores, processing that I was getting paid to do this, albeit not very much. That wasn't the point though – in my mid-20s, a desk job seemed unfathomable. I had found somewhere I thrived. I stayed on for a winter season, teaching students how to cross-country ski, as well as the history of the region's Indigenous Peoples and their use of landscape-dependent varieties of snowshoes. Winter was transformational, for both the students and me. I watched students who were new to Canada learning to skate for the first time on a frozen lake and play broomball on a meticulously flooded basketball court. I taught the importance of building a single-match fire and allowing a quinzhee, a carefully crafted snow shelter, enough time to sinter. Above all, students discovered the wonder winter could bring in Canada.

After years of wandering, I had found a place to call

home in Haliburton. My physical home was tucked offsite, a small cabin with cedar walls a stone's throw to the lake. But it felt somewhat empty. So I adopted a small red husky from a shelter in Peterborough and I named her Koona – a Cree word for snow – as she had patches of beautiful white fur to accent her ginger colouring. My hope of a consistent new running partner was short-lived; Koona was an uncharacteristically lazy husky who preferred sprawling in the shade of the large maple towering beside the cabin to joining me down the winding dirt road.

As the rhythm of the seasons repeated, I became deeply attached to both the land and the water. The centre's property encompassed more than 1,000 acres of forest abounding with trails for skiing, hiking and mountain biking, or simply getting lost in the wild with Koona. Lakes, ponds and wetlands begged to be explored; beavers, moose, bears, grouse and skunks all called the area home, making it a haven for teaching animal tracking and ecology. What better classroom is there for teaching the core subjects: science, math, social studies and history? I stayed in Haliburton for nine years, eventually becoming the centre's director and advocating the benefits of students learning outside the constraints of the traditional classroom setting.

🍁

As I sat at the dining room table with my parents two Christmases before I would make the drive to

Newfoundland, I gathered the nerve to spit out this dream I was concocting. I had made up my mind already, but having my parents' approval was important to me.

"What would you say if I told you I was thinking about running across Canada?"

A parental pause ensued.

"OK," my mother eventually managed. I had caught her off guard.

"How will you do this? Who will support you? What about Koona?" came the questions in rapid-fire succession.

These were legitimate concerns. My mother was more skeptical and perhaps more practical than my father. She knew that, if enough time passed, more than likely this dream would pass as well. Honestly, I had my own doubts. I certainly didn't have adequate answers to her numerous questions. However, my parents always gave my sisters and me the latitude to navigate our own lives. So it was with a sense of grace, mixed with apprehension, that they gave their joint response.

"Please know that whatever you choose to do, we'll love you and support you," said my dad, on their behalf.

Skeptical but supportive.

After a year of planning, second-guessing myself, having others second-guess me and training my body to run long distances daily, I packed my car, put my dog in the backseat and was ready to drive east to meet SP, a longtime friend who agreed to drive the support vehicle.

"We're *with* you," my dad said as I hugged my parents goodbye on their front yard in Winnipeg.

I knew they were with me, but I also knew they were hesitant, protective and a bit scared. They had little insight into running a marathon every day on the Trans-Canada Highway, they could not foresee the RV consistently breaking down, or how my friendship with SP would disintegrate as the kilometres slowly clicked by. Neither did I. As I set off on the first leg of my journey, driving east to St. John's, planning to retrace the kilometres on foot westward, I felt a nervous excitement. After nearly 20 years of living with this dream percolating in my subconscious, I was on my way.

CHAPTER 2

Winter on "The Rock"

> When blinding storm gusts fret thy shore
> And wild waves lash thy strand
> Thro' spindrift swirl and tempest roar
> We love thee wind-swept land
> We love thee, we love thee,
> We love thee wind-swept land.
>
> —"Ode to Newfoundland"

They call it "The Rock."

I crouched down behind some of that rock at the top of Signal Hill in St. John's, Newfoundland. A cold maritime wind with its usual bite blew in off the shores of the North Atlantic. The sky was a deep, dark blue that January morning – the kind of blue that makes it hard to frown. It was the kind of blue I had hoped for in taking my inaugural steps in my attempt to run across Canada. Looking eastward, I squinted into the bright sun, catching its glare off cresting waves headed for shore. I ducked behind the stone ledge that overlooks this vast stretch of ocean to avoid the bitter wind as I attempted to document my thoughts. I held my iPhone with an outstretched arm. I hated being in front of the camera and wondered how I could be so uncomfortable with an audience of just one. In some way, I wanted to document the start of this lifelong dream and the purpose I'd attached to it – creating a nonprofit organization, Take Me Outside, and going to as many schools as I could to engage students in the conversation about spending more time outside. I fumbled through some scattered thoughts as my bare hand turned shades of purple and orange.

I scurried back to the 1984 Chevy Citation RV, which SP and I had managed to find in Halifax just weeks before, to shed a couple of layers. I handed the phone to SP and asked her to film me as I started running down Signal Hill. For years I had daydreamed about this moment, wondering what it would be like to actually take those first steps. The finish line was incomprehensible, nine months and the equivalent of 181 marathons away. Maybe it was adrenaline; maybe it was fear, but this moment I wanted to be meaningful was short-lived. I closed the side door of the RV and came around to the front. With SP pointing the phone in my direction, I danced a little dance, half jokingly, half cringeworthy. I didn't know what I was supposed to do, so I started running.

The first 600 metres would likely be the easiest steps I took over the coming months. My legs felt fresh and strong as I ran downhill toward the downtown core of St. John's. I passed another runner who was making his way to the top of Signal Hill. I smiled ear-to-ear, wanting to stop him in his tracks and convey the significance of the moment that I was about to run across Canada. Instead, I simply kept to the unwritten code of most runners: a small raise of the hand in acknowledgement as our paths crossed.

I had a few stops to make in the first kilometre, so I knew progress would be slow. Starting on Signal Hill symbolized my own connection with nature and love for the outdoors. The lookout sits 167 metres above sea level and was built in the mid-17th century to protect St. John's from a naval attack, as well as for maritime communications up until the Second World War. Apart from its history, Signal Hill is also a place where locals and tourists come to marvel at the rugged landscape and to walk the dirt paths that wind their way through hills and rocks overlooking the Atlantic. The St. John's "green space" at Signal Hill was symbolic of my connection to the outdoors and it's where I wanted to start.

My next stop was at the small Terry Fox statue near the base of Signal Hill. SP parked the RV and joined me. I was a mere 7 years of age in 1981 when Terry Fox dipped his toe into the Atlantic and started his Marathon of Hope that would raise millions of dollars for cancer research. I was too young to fully grasp the impact he was having on Canadians as he ran 42 kilometres every day with only one good leg. In time, like most Canadians, I came to have an intimate understanding of his story. Terry Fox's legacy shaped my own desire to run across

Canada. I didn't want to duplicate his journey, yet his words and his actions inspired me, along with millions of other Canadians. If nothing else, I wanted to emulate him: his motivation, his perseverance and his desire for change. In that moment of contemplation, standing there before the stone statue of Terry Fox, I was searching for something, a blessing of sorts – a send-off from the beloved Canadian. Instead, my phone rang. It was NTV, the provincial news channel. A reporter wanted to know if I had started yet and if he could interview me for the evening news.

"I'll be dipping my toe in the Atlantic in a few minutes," I said.

"We'll be there," the reporter replied.

With that, my reflections on Terry Fox ended. I was overwhelmed, but the moment, there in front of his statue, lacked a degree of genuineness I was hoping for. I took a picture and moved on, not knowing that a more meaningful connection with the legendary Canadian was to come months later.

I couldn't dip my toe near the statue because it was fenced off to the water, so I had to run a couple of hundred metres down Water Street to find a place to safely reach the ocean. Within minutes, NTV was there with a camera in my face, deadline looming, asking quick questions that didn't have short answers. I dipped the toe of my black and silver trail shoe into the Atlantic, but the moment was sapped of its spontaneity as I had to repeat the motion several times to get the right camera angle. It was my first taste of how curated and contrived these genuine moments could be.

Then it was time for some uninterrupted running. I was scheduled to speak in the early afternoon at an elementary school 23 kilometres away in the town of Paradise. The wind nudged me along and my steps were made effortless by the excitement of starting this journey. I assured myself the scent of salt water and the squawking seagulls were real, that after so many years incubating this dream each stride actually counted, representing tangible movement west toward the Pacific. It had all the ingredients to evoke a feeling of profoundness, but didn't. All I could do was smile and tell myself this was it – this was the start of something few people had ever attempted, let alone accomplished. There are relatively few documented cases of people running across Canada; certainly fewer than 50 have run from the east coast to the west coast along the Trans-Canada Highway, the longest national highway in the world. Perhaps it's the aesthetics of it all – anyone who has driven its long stretches of asphalt can attest to its seeming bleakness at times. Those who have tried to achieve the feat of a cross-country journey without a vehicle will assure you it's a gruelling challenge, both physically and mentally. But, surprisingly, there is much beauty to be found along the way, even from this highway.

As my feet carried me outside of the downtown core of St. John's, I was filled with questions. Had I trained enough? Would our 25-year-old RV make it? What would it be like running every day on the Trans-Canada? Would anyone care what we were doing?

As I approached the school in Paradise, there were an increasing number of honked horns and waving bystanders spurring me on. Four hours after I began, I arrived in the school parking lot and ducked into the RV to change out of my sweaty running layers. SP said they were waiting for me in the gymnasium so I rushed. I didn't know exactly what to expect.

There is something alluring, or at least intriguing, about seeing someone on screen and then seeing them in real life, be they actors, athletes, musicians or politicians. I experienced this first-hand as I walked through the halls of Holy Family Elementary School that day. The teachers at the school were kind enough to repeatedly show a short video I had posted online about the run to their students in the weeks leading up to my arrival. There were shy smiles and hushed voices, students nudged friends and whispered behind cupped hands as I passed – to them, I was a minor celebrity. Six hundred students and more than 100 teachers and parents greeted me in the gymnasium. After a prolonged buildup of kind words and messages, it was my turn. I had prepared and memorized a short speech that I promptly forgot. After fumbling through a few thoughts, I resorted to an old standby: "Give me a T! Give me an A!" (It was the first and last time I would attempt to spell out the words "Take Me Outside.")

Thankfully, Emilee, a Grade 6 student, saved me. Her words eloquently summed up what I was trying to convey.

> Hello, my name is Emilee. I am a Grade 6 student at Holy Family Elementary, and I am representing the student body in my message. Today I am here to talk to you about the inspiration it is to be a part of the Take Me Outside program.
>
> My response to you is that children of Canada are spending too much time inside and not getting the right amount of outdoor activity you need every day. I believe that everyone spends too much time in front of the television, texting, playing on the computer and playing video games all day long. Instead of doing any of these indoor activities, you should be outside in the fresh air. Even a long walk with friends is a very good suggestion.
>
> Canadian lives are shortened due to the lack of daily exercise. Canadians need to learn that you need to get more than one hour of daily activity.
>
> I agree that the lives of Canadians of this generation are shortened because of the amount of indoor activity. Instead of watching TV you should go for a walk, and if you have a dog go ahead walk it! I'm sure he/she might need some

exercise too! Instead of texting, go to the park with some friends or siblings! Just get outside, have fun, be active! Come on students of Holy Family, it's our turn to get outside!

Leave it to a Grade 6 student to summarize the fundamental reason I decided to start a nonprofit organization that hoped to educate and create awareness with Canadians about this issue. I was wary that I might be one of the few who felt so strongly that Canadians, and particularly younger Canadians, were spending less time outside than previous generations. Although it's a complicated matter, Malcolm Gladwell has called screen time "one of the most troubling phenomena of our times." Town by town, city by city, I found out other people cared too. A compelling choir of voices joined me – parents, teachers and students like Emilee. We should all spend a little less time in front of screens and a little more time outside.

Easier said than done.

By my third day on the road, the adrenaline of the previous days' landmarks and interaction with students had subsided. A few kilometres south of Holyrood, I stepped onto the Trans-Canada Highway for the first time and into the first leg of focused running. Anticipation, apprehension, anxiety: they all sat heavily on my chest as I rounded the curve in the exit ramp that would spit me out on the eastbound shoulder of the Trans-Canada, facing the oncoming traffic.

Typically, if one is inclined to travel along the Trans-Canada without a vehicle, it is a summer pursuit. However, with a desire to visit as many schools as possible before the school year came to an end, I decided to start in the heart of a Canadian winter. Snowbanks hugged the shoulder as I dodged patches of black ice in my runners. I had trained on secondary highways and country roads; this was a new world of tractor-trailers and high-speed vehicles operated by bored drivers. A semi blew past so close and fast the draft from its back end momentarily threw me off balance. I had no idea if the authorities would deem it safe for me to run on the country's main thoroughfare during the winter months, into oncoming traffic, when conditions were anything but predictable. I was reluctant to ask permission for fear of someone saying no, so naivety was the name of my game. In the coming weeks, I would become somewhat accustomed to running in the wind, rain, sleet and snow of a Newfoundland winter.

As the morning progressed, I eased into a one-sided trust agreement with the drivers in the vehicles rocketing toward me. As I was never more than a metre and a half from a passing vehicle, I was able to make eye contact with each and every driver, silently attempting to plead my case for not running me over. As I made this nonverbal connection with hundreds of strangers' eyes, I realized the importance of this small connection, however brief it was. I imagined most were bewildered, thinking: What is this guy doing running on the Trans-Canada Highway in the middle of winter? On this particular day, the road was plowed wide enough to run on the gravel adjacent to the paved shoulder, which was my preference. I got some honks that day – seven to be precise – four waves and two thumbs up.

The day of running ended in the parking lot of a grocery store in Whitbourne. I went in to ask if we could park the RV overnight, and the cashier said she had seen me on the six o'clock news.

"You're the guy running! Take Me Outside, right?"

She was kind enough to let us use the outlet for the RV, which meant heat for the entire night, a luxury after several hours running in the cold.

🍁

The single largest obstacle in executing a 7600-kilometre run across the country was finding someone who would help me – a willing friend to drive the support vehicle. My criteria were fairly straightforward: someone who was willing to put their life on hold for more than half a year to drive mind-numbing stretches of the Trans-Canada Highway 50 kilometres a day and to support someone else in achieving his dream. SP was the first person I asked. She said yes.

I met SP when I moved to Haliburton to work at the outdoor education centre on the shores of Koshlong Lake. I didn't know anyone at the time, and my shyness prevented me from making friends quickly. SP took me under her wing. She had gone to camp there as a kid every summer and ultimately never left. After her degree was finished, she moved there permanently, helping to run programs throughout the school year. When I arrived, she had been there for a decade.

At first, I didn't know what to make of her. She was snarky, had an unrestrained sense of humour and a wicked tongue to go along with it. She was a fiery redhead with a temper, but everyone loved her. She was deeply empathetic and fun to be around, so people were drawn to her. And although she had numerous nicknames, most people called her "SP." My perspective on her magnetism took years to figure out, but I too was immediately drawn to her. We developed a friendship during my first few months at the outdoor centre, just as she had done with countless other staff who spent a season instructing. She made me laugh, she looked out for me and, most importantly, she took an interest in my thoughts toward outdoor education. Then, the following spring, seven months after we met, she quit. Quit her job, not the friendship (that would come later). After ten years in Haliburton, she decided to escape the bubble that often existed for staff at the centre and moved to Halifax to become a teacher.

That night, in the Whitbourne grocery store parking lot, we continued to mess about with the logistics and functionality of the Citation, its aesthetics of heavy flowered curtains and early '80s vibe another matter entirely. SP slept in the bed above at the front end of the RV. I slept on the bed at the back. SP's dog slept on what constituted the kitchen table bench, and Koona competed with me for blankets on the back bed. Koona and Sammy met for the first time a week prior to driving from Halifax to Newfoundland. Two dominant alpha females, so the first meet-and-greet did not go well. Teeth were shown, the snarls were concerning and the fear of a fight that would result in significant injuries was real. SP and I knew this going in, so the contingency plan was pretty straightforward. Separate the two dogs in the RV with a baby gate: Sammy in the front, Koona in the back. For the first few weeks, a keen eye was needed to make sure they wouldn't leap over or test the boundaries of this set-up. But in time they both seemed to become apathetic toward each other.

❦

In the first four days, I ran a total of 103.6 kilometres, without a shower. The Citation came equipped with a toilet and shower, but as it was winter, we couldn't use it because the pipes would freeze. The washroom quickly became a much-needed storage closet, which easily took precedence over cleanliness. After a shortened day of running due to snow, we found the home of the Fudges, friends of my parents in Arnold's Cove, who invited us for dinner. I shoved spoonfuls of homemade chili into my mouth while SP held the conversation. The Fudges shared with us their own stories of spending time outside as kids in rural Newfoundland. Connecting with the land and water was an integral part of being a Newfoundlander. After my stomach declared nothing else would fit, SP and I took turns showering. I watched the trail of hard-earned mud and dirt swirl down the drain and contemplated the scarcity of these amenities in the coming months. I savoured the warm foggy haze of the Fudges' bathroom for what was likely too long.

Each stride along the Trans-Canada Highway – the TCH I was beginning to call it – was moving me westward, albeit slowly. Each town, city or truck stop was a welcome sight: Clarenville, Port Blandford, Terra Nova National Park, Glovertown – the homemade pie at the Irving Station in Goobies made those countless strides worthwhile. But on Day 13, within the first few kilometres, there was a stabbing pain on the outside of my right knee. I looked down at my knee in hopes of discerning what was wrong, but this was a new pain. I called it quits after nine kilometres and SP picked me up. We reluctantly drove the 40 kilometres to Gander so I could rest for a couple of days. I would later discover the pain was a common running injury, a tight iliotibial (IT) band.

The snow started as we pulled into the city limits of Gander. By the time I curled up in bed next to Koona in the parking lot of a Walmart, there were 20 centimetres on the ground. The immensity of the task at hand added weight to the mass of blankets I lay under. In just shy of two weeks, I had run 287.2 kilometres, which in the context of running was significant. But, with 632 kilometres to go to reach the ferry in Port aux Basques on the west end of Newfoundland, I wondered if I could make it to the other end of this province, let alone the country. Thankfully, drifting off to sleep saved me from having to answer.

I was jarred awake at 4 a.m. by a symphony of beeps. What I drowsily imagined to be an alarm clock was actually the incessant beeping of snowplows reversing. It pierced the thin exterior of our home. The only respite came when the plows moved forward, giant pieces of metal scraping the cement clear of snow. This continued for hours, cheating me of needed sleep. For the next day and a half, we did laundry, I stretched my IT band and we spent endless hours in Walmart, walking the aisles, using the indoor plumbing and, most importantly, staying warm under the glare of fluorescent lights. Heat had become an issue in the RV. There was a furnace, but it required propane – and not the kind that comes in a canister or a tank. This RV required a special hose to fill up its tank and there were limited places to find such a hookup. We were assured of the proper set-up in Grand Falls–Windsor, but that was five or six days down the road. Our temporarily stationary home at Walmart forced us to try out multiple plug-in heaters so we didn't burn through our low supply of propane. This required numerous trips back and forth between the store and the RV before we finally decided on one. If we sat right in front of the last heater we tried, we could warm our hands and faces. Sold.

After two rest days and another school visit, it was time to get back on the highway. My IT band felt looser as I took those tentative first few strides. But east of Gander I ducked off the shoulder to relieve myself. While navigating some bushes, I clumsily pulled a muscle in my left leg, and then shin splints set in. So back to Gander we went for another couple of days of rest. Walmart had lost its appeal, so we found a cheap hotel. On the first night, I enjoyed a real bed and the room to myself as SP stayed in the RV. On the second night we switched. Having a break from one another in the confined space of the RV took precedence over the amenities of a shared hotel room. The next morning, SP came out to the RV to discover a flat tire. Hours in Walmart were replaced by hours at the mechanic. As we drove away with a patched tire, SP clipped the garage roof. The Citation ended up with several new holes near the back and the stripping near the top was half ripped off. The RV's woes would prove to be a metaphor: no matter how noble the intent, relationships can be difficult and can incur minor damages, especially crammed into a tight space in the damp chilly days of a Newfoundland winter.

The province felt bigger than I anticipated, and as the days turned into weeks, I was getting slower and slower. My knee continued to nag me, and although there were some good days among the bad, the ferry in Port aux Basques that would deliver us from the island to the mainland may as well have been on the dark side of the moon.

Day 21 was a bright spot, however, with snow starting to fall in the morning and becoming quite heavy by mid-afternoon. Koona loved the snow, so it didn't take much convincing to rouse her out of her cozy spot in the RV, nestled between blankets on my bed. Together we walked and ran the Trans Canada Trail that hugged the highway. It was one of the few times throughout the trip that Koona could join me. She loved burying her nose in the snow and rolling on her back, making the best snow dog angels she could. That day I also didn't have to contend with traffic. My eyes wandered to the tall pines surrounding me, a welcome change from endlessly scanning the highway for oncoming semi-trailers.

The students at the schools we visited energized me. It was difficult to know the full extent to which sharing my story of running across Canada and talking to them about spending time outside would have an impact, but a belief in this greater goal was beginning to take shape and that alone pushed me.

On Day 26, I ran 42.2 kilometres, my first marathon distance. It was a good day, but our glass was feeling perpetually half-empty: the good days seemed short-lived, while the trying days were a constant. On Valentine's Day, our generator that was primarily used for heat – when we could find propane – wouldn't start. And, within the first ten kilometres of running, my knee was hurting again. But with school visits lined up, there was pressure to keep moving forward. Running became a walk/run combination on the TCH. After a quick sandwich piled high with turkey, vegetables and hummus, I set out again and soon enough, as was the established pattern, the RV passed me. Minutes later, I looked up and saw the Citation, severely tilted off the highway. SP had hit a soft shoulder and the tires had slipped into the ditch. As I drew closer, SP was standing to the side, assessing.

"Well, that doesn't look good," I said with a smile, trying not to make her feel bad.

"Stupid," she responded. "What a stupid move."

"Everything's OK inside though?" I asked.

"Dogs are fine. Some dishes came crashing down. But it's fine."

A friendly Newfoundlander (is there any another kind?) stopped to see if we were OK. A tow truck was en route, so we were fine. As he pulled away, he too hit the soft shoulder and now both vehicles were stuck. We were hours away from being helped, but with the dogs calm and the RV relatively intact I decided to keep running. SP would find me when she could. By the end of the day, I had run and walked 47 kilometres. We drove to Deer Lake, a small community that sat on the north end of a lake by the same name, where the snow was falling fast and furious. By the time I collapsed from exhaustion, the accumulation was knee-deep. Cupid was nowhere to be found.

🍁

Each morning I woke to the sight of my breath hanging

in the sub-zero air. I lay cocooned under layers of sleeping bags and blankets with Koona curled up close by. Although a husky, she pined for my body heat as much as I needed hers. Peeking my head out, eyes still heavy with sleep, I had developed an acute sense of how cold it would be when I crawled out from my blankets and into the day. Attempting to look out the frosted windows of the RV was futile; I already knew it was a sea of white.

My desire to expose more than just my face to the frigid air was equal to my desire to lace up my shoes and run 40 to 50 kilometres. But establishing routines was paramount to reaching the Pacific Ocean. I was learning to reject all the "what ifs." *What if I just sleep for another half an hour? What if I take the morning off and run this afternoon? What if I take today off and maybe tomorrow's weather will be nicer? What if I just can't do this anymore?*

As the layers of cold damp running clothes hit my skin, I was jolted awake. On the single burner stove, I toasted bagel slices and lathered them with half-frozen peanut butter. On cue, Koona's head would pop out from the covers. Peanut butter surpassed warmth and she knew I was a sucker for her pleading eyes. Lined rubber boots were always the first footwear I donned in the morning as I opened the door into the not-so-early morning. Koona pushed past me and scurried around sniffing for a spot to pee on the perimeter of the parking lot we called home last night. I made a feeble attempt at an internal pep talk while I waited. *You've got this, Colin.*

Forty kilometres today and in seven days you'll be at the ferry and on your way to Nova Scotia. My own words of encouragement fell flat. The 41 kilometres I would run that day were a drop in the ocean, Victoria was still more than 7000 kilometres, and I predicted, 250 parking lot sleeps away.

After Koona finished her business, it was my turn. Into the RV she went, and back out into the quiet morning I would go, searching for a secluded bush or tree to hide behind. I began to care less and less who saw me. Squatting with the cold winter hitting my bare buttocks, I surveyed the area half-heartedly for morning walkers or drivers.

By the time I would return to the RV, SP was usually up, her green wool sweater a constant, making tea. Once boots were replaced with shoes, there was little room for further procrastination. I would run for two to three hours in the morning, and SP would find somewhere to park within that range for me to break and have lunch.

"Twenty to 25?" she asked, referring to kilometres.

"Yep."

Once we had our routine established, those were precisely how many words were exchanged each morning.

The first argument with SP came within the first three weeks of starting the run. Ours was a friendship that seemed to excel at finding lows rather than highs; there had been many arguments over the years. Yet, inexplicably, it felt like a strong friendship, at least most of the time. As our confined RV life was settling in, our familiar pattern reared its head one evening. I wrote and dedicated my daily blog to SP – my support team, working behind the scenes in unglamorous conditions. SP would not only be helping me for months to come but she also helped me get to the start line after a year of planning together. I wanted readers and her to know that this would all fall apart without her, even though her desire to stay in the background was made clear. I wrote about her willingness to give to others, and how she knows when to listen, and when to retort and tell you to suck it up. Her love for Sammy was unforgiving and her abilities as a teacher were inspiring. I told her about the post after I finished writing it.

"Thanks. I think I'll skip that one," she said.

"Why?" I asked, confused.

"I'm not interested."

"I said nice things about you."

"Don't want to read it."

Like my mother, I wear my emotions on my sleeve, and was unable to bury the oversensitivity I felt at her response. I couldn't seem to let it go. I kept pressing while she kept deflecting. Eventually, the frustration of not getting the response I hoped for ended in silence. For years I had lived on my own but now found myself sharing this small space with a friend who maddened me. Going to bed that night was painstakingly hard. I was prone to being on the spectrum of wanting to resolve tough conversations. SP was not. I lay in bed stewing, too stubborn to apologize or to simply let it go.

The next day, it was back to business. Emotions were cooled by the winter air, dog cuddles and the shared anticipation of getting off this island of rock. Corner Brook to the ferry at Port aux Basques was the homestretch. A 200-kilometre homestretch to officially finish the first province, but a homestretch nonetheless.

Determination fuelled my first few strides that morning. *This is becoming familiar and comfortable.* Within 15 kilometres, discomfort set in, my right knee again betraying me. At the 25-kilometre mark I had to stop. I was in more pain than I had experienced at any other point in the last three weeks. I sat on the side of the highway, gutted, waiting for SP to pick me up. My mind raced, searching for a solution – a decision had to be made. If I went back to Corner Brook, a medical professional would tell me to rest. The alternative was to carry on, but forego the running part and walk until my knee felt better. SP arrived, her eyes uncertain at the sight of me sitting on the side of the road, again. I laid out our options, hoping for direction. Sometimes it's easier when someone else tells you what to do. SP wanted nothing of it. Her goal of getting off this island of rock was abundantly clear and equal to mine, but she would support either decision I made, heading back for rest or continuing to move forward.

Injuries can be a strange thing. When I ran forward, my IT band was tight and the pain in my knee was sharp. I could run sideways and even backwards without any pain, but although I had tried this for short stretches along the highway, it wasn't an effective way of getting from point A to point B. When I walked, there was no pain whatsoever. When I walked, it felt like I had two strong, healthy legs. For 20 years, I had dreamed of running across Canada and I had trained hard to get where I was. I had envisioned *running* across Canada, not walking.

"I think I'll just have to try walking this afternoon, so I might take quite a bit longer," I concluded.

"Roger that."

After wolfing down a sandwich and some chocolate, I headed back out; shoulders slumped, and began walking. I enjoyed meandering a thoughtful stroll through the moments of life, but one does not meander among the traffic on the Trans-Canada Highway. I had to keep my pace up to make it bearable. Walking with the weight of my thoughts seemed even heavier than they would with running. I hated the idea of walking for days on end. *This was not my intention or part of my dream!* But rationalization came to my defense: ultra-trail runners, those who run 50- to 150-kilometre races, will all tell you there comes a time in the race when they have to walk. Usually it's up a hill, or several hills. They walk to give their legs a rest, yet they are still considered to have run their race. Running 7600 kilometres over nine months was my own ultra-race of sorts. And if I needed to walk a couple of hundred kilometres of this race, I could live with that.

Newfoundland would not release its grip on us. With

less than 100 kilometres to go to the ferry, high winds and blowing snow prevented me from running again. The next day, it cleared enough to attempt the TCH. There was little traffic to be found and for good reason. At midday SP handed me a peanut butter sandwich out of the RV window because she couldn't find anywhere to stop due to the sheer amount of snow. Later that afternoon, I received a text.

SP: The battery is dead.
Me: Should I keep going?
SP: Yep, I'll figure it out.

And she did. After four boosts and a hazard-light escort to the town of Doyles, it turned out the alternator belt had broken and was draining the battery. This in turn caused engine trouble, which blew the muffler out. Another chilly night without propane awaited us as the dogs made it difficult to accept the invitation we received for a warm bed inside. And, ironically, we felt most at home in our treasonous box on wheels. The next morning, we were back at it, a new belt for the Citation and I was off to a running start. We were hell-bent on catching the ferry in two days.

Determination was at the forefront in my psyche as I set out for what I hoped would be my last full day of running in Newfoundland. If all went according to plan, I'd only have to squeak out seven kilometres on the last morning before boarding the ferry, decidedly concluding my first province. I walked but felt strong and every few minutes began to break into a running stride. The knee pain had momentarily vanished. I was scared of feeling that knife in the side of my knee, so I kept forcing myself to walk. But each time I would begin to run, it was consistently pain-free.

Not long after I set out, a large, orange sign appeared in the distance. As I got closer, I could make out the word "Caution." A little closer and I could see the rest of its message: "Winds in this area have been recorded to gust in excess of 200 km/h." That stretch of the Trans-Canada Highway is known as the Wreckhouse, infamous for its winds known to blow train cars off track and flip semi-trailers like fallen leaves. It was also one of the most beautiful stretches of highway I had yet encountered. As I ran west, mountains towered on my left, their snow-capped peaks contrasting vividly against the brilliant blue of the sky. On my right, the dark-blue ocean pummelled a stretch of rocky coast. The legendary wind did not disappoint, it blew hard from the north, forcing me to lean toward the lane of traffic to combat its force. I pulled out my phone and snapped two selfies. I wanted to share the wild, unyielding beauty of this island and ocean with those following my journey.

It seems as though our relationship with the outdoors is, ironically, reflected most through social media these days. Going for a family hike, climbing a mountain or simply going for a run around the neighbourhood is no longer a stand-alone activity. They are often accompanied by numerous hashtags and filters that attempt to capture the beauty or the experience that surrounds us. The justification is that we hope to inspire others to get outside and find the same adventures – find the same beauty. It increasingly feels like inspiring others really isn't the true intention of posting curated photos on Instagram anymore. We have omitted the stories that include the mundane: the routines and the speed bumps that are everyday life. Without establishing patterns and experiencing the monotony of running on the shoulder of the TCH day in and day out, my dream of running across this country would have proven futile.

*

On March 3, after 44 days of battling cold winter nights, endless RV issues, very little money and a finicky IT band, I woke up the happiest I had felt in weeks. I hadn't slept much the night before; ceaseless winds violently shook the Citation. We had spent the night in the parking lot of a Tim Hortons and, after a morning muffin and the use of a toilet, I was ready to start the day.

As I headed back to the RV, I sensed something wasn't right, a sixth sense I could feel in my gut. Sure enough, there was a flat tire at the front of the RV. I looked at the sky for strength and exhaled, a long, tired exhale. There was another flat at the back of the RV. Two flat tires. The ferry was scheduled to leave in five hours.

We put enough air in the tires with our compressor to get it over to Canadian Tire, and then I organized a ride back to the previous day's finish line. I hoped by the time I ran the seven kilometres to the ferry terminal, the RV would be there, ready to go. But, my short mileage completed, the Citation was nowhere to be found. Despite our desperate pleas – which did produce two mechanics for the job – it still took more than four hours to change both tires. We pulled into the terminal just as the ferry drifted out. We had missed it by sheer minutes. We would end up having to wait until early the next morning to catch our ride to Nova Scotia and back to mainland Canada. Tears slipped over my cheeks.

I sat alone in the ferry terminal, while SP napped in the RV. I was heartsick and elated. Elated I had run 919.2 kilometres across Newfoundland and spoken with 2,300 students, but I felt defeated by the missed ferry. It felt crushing to wait another 17 hours. As I sat and waited, I began to catch up on emails. I read one from my dad; he had spent his morning with seven new refugees who had found a safe haven in Winnipeg. One of the refugees was a woman from Afghanistan. She had come to Canada because the Taliban shot and killed her husband and two brothers. Suddenly, slogging through winter on The Rock paled in comparison, and getting upset over missing the ferry was unjustified. Perspective is important in such moments.

CHAPTER 3

Learning Outside

We learn much more from the world around us than we necessarily do sitting at desks.

—Sir Ken Robinson

Rough seas made for little sleep after the ferry departed Port aux Basques in the early hours of the morning as I tossed and turned on the disco-themed decor of the lounge chairs. Escaping the island overshadowed the accomplishment and experience of the last several weeks. It would be months before I could properly process the impact left by the people and my connection to the wild waves and windswept land.

As the ferry approached North Sydney, on Nova Scotia's Cape Breton Island, the skies cleared and the waters calmed. Stepping onto the mainland rejuvenated both SP and me. It had been weeks since we had smiled at each other, and a sense of relief was shared that we could celebrate together. As we stared back at the ocean and the docked ferry, I wondered if the worst was behind us. The beginning of March would usher in warmer temperatures and blooming flowers – a visible rebirth throughout the natural environment. Perhaps there could be a rebirth of sorts in the beige box on wheels we called home.

The sun warmed me that morning as I took my first strides of Day 47. The stillness of the pines that lined the highway imparted a calmness and serenity as I passed. That calmness was needed as the Citation continued to be difficult. We found the correct nozzle for propane at a nearby Canadian Tire in Sydney, but on that day it wasn't working properly. In that moment, we decided to give up on heat, with people assuring us that spring in Nova Scotia was just around the corner. Both tires still needed work, but for now they were full of air and keeping us on course.

Cape Breton Island is a masterpiece of geology and continental drift. Over millions of years, three separate landscapes came together in what seems an unlikely coincidence. The northwest tip of the island is made up of the oldest rock in the Atlantic provinces, coming from the collision of continental plates that resulted in the supercontinent Rodinia. It is the same rock found in the Canadian Shield in Labrador, Quebec, Ontario and Nunavut. Most of the northern half of the island is the Bras d'Or Terrane, made up of sedimentary and volcanic rock that began forming on what is now considered South America. And the southern part of the island, the Avalon Terrane, is volcanic rock that formed and then broke off of what is now Africa. These three tectonic plates merged to create what many consider one of the most beautiful islands in the world, with its rugged cliffs, rocky shores and rolling farmland, along with glacial valleys, mountains and plateaus. I remember looking out from Wreck Cove years earlier as I drove the Cabot Trail, feeling the power of the ocean crashing into those rocky shores below. Breathtaking beauty is gifted to those who visit this landscape. But is there something greater at work when looking out over this immense ocean? If we allow natural experiences to grip us, are we not then shaped by the land and water, by the quest for answers and the resulting introspection?

That first day on Cape Breton, I ran more than 47 kilometres through jaw-dropping scenery and my legs felt strong. It also marked a milestone – since dipping my toe into the Atlantic, I had run more than 1000 kilometres. With 6500 kilometres still ahead of us, the milestone came and went unacknowledged, except by my mom, who had recently sent a note that contained a quote by American Rabbi Irwin Kula, perfect for the unsung moment: "Enough is not simply about being satisfied with what we have, it's about feeling the fullness of the partial." I tried in earnest to feel that fullness.

SP made fajitas for dinner while Koona and Sammy patiently waited for fallen scraps under the foldaway table, which acted as a catchall for any activity that required sitting. The conversation was light that evening, as we discussed a recent email from our mutual friend Matt. For the last couple of years, Matt had lived and worked in Yukon in a government job that put his degree in biology to use. The previous evening, he had sat in a local community centre with about 35 people to discuss wildlife conservation and management in Yukon, listening to locals, trappers and Indigenous people share their concerns across the territory. SP and I reflected on Matt's uplifting words.

The meeting got underway and the conversation started in immediately with incentives for trappers, because it currently isn't worth their while. Consensus was that there are too many predators, which means not enough moose for local people to harvest. After much input from attendees, and deliberations about extended seasons, costs of trapping, the high intelligence of wolves and their intricate social behaviours, an Elder spoke. He spoke very softly, you could've heard a pin drop for sure. Everyone leaned in to listen. He said, "People just don't get out on the land as much as they used to." I immediately thought of you guys and your adventure and your challenges and the immensity of your task and the enormity of your vision really hit home.

The next day, as I lay under the covers on my plywood bed, Koona curled up in the crook of my knee, I could hear the snow melting from the tree branches. The ice was starting to recede from the unpaved shoulder on the edge of the TCH. Instead of the crisp and crunchy strike of my shoes on the frozen ground, each stride started to have a squish to it. I was ecstatic to feel the warmth of the sun on my face. My legs were rejuvenated as well – for the third consecutive day I ran a marathon distance. My excitement was tempered, knowing the unlikelihood of winter releasing its grasp on the east coast this early, but the anticipation of spring was at least in the air. Within days, the highway was virtually free of snow, and my feet revelled in the feeling of small pebbles on the shoulder. It was a runner's paradise compared to the solid, monotonous pavement.

Eight kilometres into Day 51, a car pulled over and stopped on the shoulder ahead of me. Rob, a teacher from Halifax I had connected with the previous week, hopped out, followed by Jennifer and her daughters Fleur and Blythe, whom Rob had taught. Rob looked the part of a runner, with spandex tights, a visor and sunglasses. All four were wearing Take Me Outside T-shirts and had driven two and a half hours from Halifax to run alongside me. Rob had been following our progress since we first started out in Newfoundland and was a strong supporter and advocate of our message. It was the first time someone had joined me to run on the TCH, and I was apprehensive about having enough conversation to fill the long stretch of highway ahead. But, as we shuffled our way west over the next hour and a half, I enjoyed the companionship of a kindred spirit. Rob and I both loved curling and had owned Volkswagen camper vans in our youth. We chatted with ease as my initial apprehension faded.

After 14 kilometres, Jennifer traded with Rob and we continued on to Antigonish as the soft morning light filtered through a thin layer of cloud. The frequency of vehicles travelling 100 kilometres per hour was not entirely conducive to conversation, but Jennifer didn't seem to notice. Her smile was infectious as she shared her plan to commit 40 philanthropic acts in honour of turning 40 years old. More kilometres fell away while we chatted.

Once we arrived in town, Fleur and Blythe joined in for a kilometre, finishing at Tim Hortons for a sandwich and glazed donuts. Then we showed the girls the RV and introduced them to Koona and Sammy. They politely insisted the RV didn't smell despite seven weeks of sweaty running clothes and numerous missed showers. As we said goodbye, Rob handed me a stack of letters his students had written for us.

"Today has been really inspiring," Rob said.

Jennifer and her kids gave SP and me big hugs as we said goodbye.

Later that evening, I sat with the letters piled on my lap. Our message had resonated with these kids. Rob's students wrote to tell us they were grateful for our efforts and shared what activities they liked doing outside. I hoped our message was directly affecting their habits. This was the nourishment I needed, knowing they fully believed in what we were trying to accomplish, compelling me to continue putting one foot in front of the other.

The next day, Day 52, my legs had little interest in helping me finish the sixth marathon in seven days. My IT band had flared up again at the end of yesterday's run, which meant the evening was spent with the foam roller on the floor, Koona and Sammy becoming accustomed to this practice. Fighting through gasps, grunts and tears, I absorbed the long-term benefit of the short-term pain. The RV was in rough shape too. The brake lights and turning signals were no longer working, so the next day, after dropping me off at my start point for the day, SP drove to New Glasgow to have the issue fixed. Her patience was saintly.

By ten kilometres, my legs weren't interested in running any further. But SP was in New Glasgow so I had little choice but to keep moving. By 20 kilometres, I was eagerly awaiting a text to say she was on her way. It didn't come. By 25 kilometres, I was cold, hungry and my body wanted to stop. At 30 kilometres, I took an exit from the highway. The only solace nearby was a parking lot of what seemed to be abandoned tractor-trailers – no trucks attached and most looked like they had been sitting for quite some time. I sat underneath one of the trailers, hugged up against a set of wheels, frustrated and chilled to the bone. Pulling my hoodie over my head, I sat dejected, wondering when SP would text to say she was on her way. Within view of the TCH, I watched vehicles pass by, wanting desperately to be anywhere other than where I was.

My physical woes were a gentle breeze compared to

those of Canadian folk artist Maud Lewis. Growing up in rural Nova Scotia in the early 1900s, she suffered from rheumatoid arthritis and other physical ailments that left her hunched over. Her family was poverty-stricken growing up and this poverty continued into adulthood. At the age of 34, Lewis married a fish monger and farm labourer, and from a one-room cabin, now sitting inside the Art Gallery of Nova Scotia, Lewis painted numerous playful outdoor scenes: idyllic coves, winter sleigh rides, skiers, sledders, deer, oxen and cats. Although not part of her daily surroundings, it was these memories from childhood and her time outside that provided some of her inspiration to paint. In severe hardship, she found comfort in the outdoors, including the sometimes harsh winters of the east coast. There is a time for cozying up inside and hibernating from the bitter cold that can blow through the Maritimes. There is also happiness, laughter and fulfillment to be found in the winter months.

With my hands tucked in my armpits for warmth, I shivered, teeth clattering, waiting for the Citation to appear from my unlikely spot underneath the tractor-trailer. There wasn't much laughter in that moment. Little did I know that, after four attempts, SP finally found a dealership that had time to look at the RV. She waited all afternoon, discovering the wiring had been altered – a home remedy that required a complete undoing in order to redo.

"Could anything else go wrong with this piece of junk?"

she asked when she finally arrived. I was too cold and frustrated to respond, but in time the answer would be yes. Thankfully, the next day was a day off from the road. The RV was fixed and I found a shower at the local YMCA – my first in nine days.

🍁

On Day 55, SP and I were on the cusp of a week-long break. A break from running, but maybe, more importantly, a break from each other. For almost two months, we had shared cramped quarters, with each other and with our fur enemies – keeping the dogs separated in the RV still required constant attention. My days had a singular purpose driven by one simple goal: to run as much as I could. SP's days were spent shuttling the RV forward 20 to 25 kilometres in the morning, sitting and waiting, then shuffling the RV forward another 20 to 25 kilometres in the afternoon, all the while dealing with its decrepit idiosyncrasies. Whatever notions of life on the road either of us had conjured up months earlier, moving in 25-kilometre increments, although a reality, was not what we had envisioned.

Nineteen kilometres was all I had to push through to reach Truro before heading south to Halifax. Perhaps a change in direction from something other than westward would prove beneficial. I tried to stop my mind from informing my body we were on the cusp of a break, but my mind faltered, closely followed by my body. Each kilometre felt longer than the last. The sideways rain didn't help in passing the time any quicker. It was an unpleasant reminder of how a weak mind can affect the physical body. It felt like hours before I broke my pedestrian pace and hobbled into the RV in Truro. I was sopping wet, so it was a relief to change into dry clothes. But my relief was short-lived upon discovering we had our fourth flat tire in seven weeks. It was 5 p.m. and every mechanic in Truro was closed, forcing us to drive to Halifax. We headed south in small increments, stopping regularly to pump up the tire, hoping it would last another few kilometres until the next gas station. When we finally made it to Halifax, we were physically and mentally exhausted.

SP's mom lived in downtown Halifax, and within minutes of parking in a grocery store lot close by, SP had her things packed and was headed for a warm shower and the comfort of her mom's home with Sammy. The joy of having 125 square feet of living space to myself couldn't be overstated. Koona and I strolled aimlessly that evening, unaware of what direction we were going. After unnecessary amounts of deep-fried carbs were consumed, I crawled into bed. Koona shifted on the blankets and buried her head into my shoulder. For a moment, my mind darted sporadically, bouncing from one thought to the next. Then it sunk in that I was alone. Although surrounded by late-night shoppers and the faint hum of fluorescent lights above, I was the only human in the confine of those panelled walls. Bliss.

🍁

The week in Halifax was a welcome change from our usual routine of running and driving. We both knew several teachers in the Halifax area, and SP had herself taught just over the Macdonald Bridge in Dartmouth. After a visit to Southdale Elementary in the morning, and some excited primary students who excelled at tag, we headed to Bicentennial School in the afternoon where SP had taught on and off for the past couple of years. Adoring students mobbed the deserving, anonymous supporter of this journey. I was hopeful this might re-energize SP, seeing familiar faces and having her be the centre of attention instead of me. After a short chat with the Grade 9 students, we headed outside with them for a neighbourhood walk. Shuffling around was much quieter with the Grade 9s and a stark contrast from the energy and enthusiasm of the primary students we had visited that morning. I asked them what changed in their relationship with the outdoors between Grade 2 and Grade 9, trying to account for their subdued demeanour.

"What's fun in Grade 2 is obviously different in Grade 9," one student remarked.

In Ken Robinson's popular TED talk about the education system, *Do Schools Kill Creativity*, he makes the argument that we educate students *out* of creativity, with the focus in school more toward math and science and less on the arts. We're all born creative. Kids are given crayons and art supplies and asked to create the world they both imagine and see around them. Somehow, on the journey to adulthood, the majority of us often lose that creativity. Is the same true for the time we spend outside? Kids love being outside when they're young. By the time the teenage years are reached, it often seems less desirable. Perhaps it's because our "fun" activities as we grow older include more technology, which keeps us inside. Although we'd be hard-pressed to find Grade 9s playing tag at school, or adults frolicking about on their lunch breaks, that simple game of tag we played that morning was a reminder of how simple it can be.

❦

"The function of education is to teach one to think intensively and to think critically. Intelligence plus character – that is the goal of true education," said Martin Luther King Jr. Yet the *how* and *where* of formal education often takes precedence over the *why*. Charming small schoolhouses have shifted into large, bleak institutions, but one constant has remained during the 150 years of formalized education: students sitting, at a desk, surrounded by four walls. It wasn't always that way though. For thousands of years, traditional education within Indigenous communities had the same purpose – the same *why* as our modern education system. Children were taught on the land; they learned experientially how to hunt and to fish and acquired the skills needed to meet the demands within their territory. It was real world experience that shaped the values of their people. Elders, parents and the community shared stories about these values and how best to interact with their environment, while physically immersed in it. Today, students are removed from the natural environment, and many adults are too, tucked away at desks in concrete and steel buildings. Certainly stories meant for learning are still shared with students today, but a lot of the time it comes sitting at a desk. At the worst of times, these stories at school are shared only through YouTube or some other online platform.

We have been led to believe that technology will revolutionize education. We have marched forward with blinders on, equipping classrooms with SMART boards, making sure every student has a laptop and, in most schools, letting students be distracted by the phones they carry in their pockets. Yet there is little research that supports students learning more effectively through technology. In fact, studies have shown students are more likely to remember things better when taking notes by hand rather than on a laptop. The myth of multitasking is prevalent, and the misperception that productivity can be increased on multiple devices looms large, yet we seem intent on using as many devices as possible to educate. Perhaps we're all so drawn in by the potential we want to see rather than what actually exists. And the paradox is that the traditional way of educating students – hands-on, outdoors and on the land – still shows the most benefits, as outlined by Liz

Kirk and Grant Linney, two long-standing members of the Council of Outdoor Educators of Ontario.

Outdoor and Environmental Education's (OEE) real-life, hands-on approach significantly broadens and deepens learning leading to more engagement and enthusiasm, increased proficiency in language skills as well as science, technology, engineering and mathematics (STEM), and improved skills in critical thinking. Its highly interactive nature spurs the significant development of both personal and interpersonal growth. Character traits such as creativity, self-motivation, assertiveness and resilience are enhanced. Social skills are also developed; these include co-operation, effective communication, decision-making and problem solving. Outdoor learning educates for physical and mental wellbeing. Research shows that time spent outdoors leads to a marked reduction in anxiety and an increased ability to perform positively in the face of adversity. Time in natural settings also correlates with increased physical activity and fitness in children, as well as the potential lifelong adoption of healthy and sustainable outdoor pursuits. Other improvements in wellbeing include reduction in the symptoms of attention deficit disorder as well as in high school dropout and crime rates.

OEE educates for environment. Where passive screen time dominates, outdoor education provides powerful first-hand encounters with our natural surroundings, a key first step toward developing a much-needed lifelong ethic for a healthy and sustainable future.

While technology can enhance and complement a student's educational experience, can there be an acceptance that it is not the saviour with respect to thinking intensively and critically? If intelligence and character are the true goals of education, as Martin Luther King Jr. stated, surely there is room for that to be achieved outside four walls and a desk.

🍁

SP had joined me for most of the school visits throughout our week in Halifax, but outside of those times, I didn't see her. We needed a break from each other, but I was uneasy about how things would be once we got back on the TCH. In theory, we would be in each other's company for another five months; a debrief felt warranted before tackling another stretch of this project. So, a few days before we would head back out on the road, I asked if she wanted to take the dogs for a walk. We met in Point Pleasant Park in the southern end of the city. Peppered with white birch, red maples and a network of trails, the park has endless opportunities for outdoor adventure: bike rides, slow winter runs, first dates, family walks and difficult conversations. It was the latter I anticipated as we met at the north end near the shipping yard. SP's reclusiveness had increased as we inched further west on the road and our communication was breaking down – was I the cause of this? If I was, what could I do to fix it? What did she need in order to find some degree of joy on our journey?

I was prepared for reluctance and continued silence but was instead met with a big smile. The time off with family and friends seemed to have been exactly what was needed. We walked and laughed and even joked about how long Newfoundland took. I felt we had turned a tight corner with our friendship that made broaching some of the unresolved issues seem out of place. The walk was the first time we had done anything as friends in a while that didn't entail a supporting role. Our on-the-road routines had been established and, aside from dinner, most everything was done separately: SP driving, me running, SP reading, me blogging, SP fixing the RV, me responding to emails. The cramped walls of the RV had taken a toll and this park allowed us space to breathe. The fresh air and happy dogs – when separated – were a hopeful sign of a new chapter in the journey.

Forty-eight hours later we were back on the road, heading north toward the Trans-Canada, the pleasant walk in the park a distant memory. The RV felt thick with resentment. Uttered words were few and far between in the Citation as we drove up Highway 102. It was difficult to leave the comfort and beauty of Halifax behind, and for SP, friends and family even more so. She silently stared past the windshield, a woman of her word – she had committed to supporting me for six months and wanted to fulfill her commitment regardless of the personal hardship. It would be months before she gave in. In silence, we merged back onto the Trans-Canada.

My legs were sluggish as I reacquainted myself with the shoulder of the TCH. I covered 23 kilometres on the first day back, but struggled through six the next day. I couldn't run 200 metres without considerable pain on the outside of my right knee. After eight days of rest, and two excruciatingly deep massages during which I could feel the IT band release, I was deeply frustrated to still be in such pain. I stood on the side of the highway and screamed at the sky as vehicles sped past, oblivious to my torment. *How can I run another 6000 kilometres like this? How can I fix this? Is this a sign this lifelong dream might end up short-lived?* Doubt is the devil and it filled me to the brim. From lack of funding to RV issues to the physical toll, it was the first time I truly considered quitting. In the year leading up to the run I had prepared myself for this possibility, logically if not emotionally. Head down, I debated whether to retreat to Halifax to reassess, or to continue on, even if it meant walking.

I turned away from the road as tears streamed down my face. I texted SP and she quickly found me. I knew it was my decision, but I wanted her to be part of it. In fact, part of me wanted her to make the decision for me. I hoped that her desire to go back to her friends and family might tip the scale of indecision.

"This is up to you Colin," she said, as we sat in the parked RV. "I'll support whatever you decide."

I kneeled down at my bed and gave Koona a rub on her ears, fighting the procrastination of making a decision.

As I stepped back outside, the whoosh of passing vehicles resumed. I closed the RV door behind me, clinching my decision. For the first few minutes, I walked, my brain in problem-solving mode. *How could I alleviate this pain?* I picked up my pace – not a sprint, but more of a ten-kilometre-an-hour pace, a pace I had run consistently over 17 years. The pace I had adopted over the last couple of months was about as slow as one could imagine to still be considered running. It was necessary in order to save my body for 7600 kilometres. But, in slowing down, my stride had unknowingly changed. I had honestly never focused on the mechanics of good running, so I relied solely on muscle memory as I quickened my stride. Miraculously, the remaining 15 kilometres were pain-free, albeit with numerous walking breaks. The next day, I plowed through 39 kilometres without a hint of discomfort. My hamstrings weren't the happiest muscles in my body, but they held together and I felt a renewed sense of strength and determination as we neared Quebec.

CHAPTER 4

Spring Awakening

The wetness began to seep through my running socks as my shoes splattered through slush and wet snow. My black running pants were holding up, a minor miracle considering I had worn the same pair every running day since starting in Newfoundland more than two months ago. Thankfully, they were loose fitting and not spandex tight; I had always been self-conscious of my skinny, chicken-like legs. Underneath, I wore a pair of running shorts – the kind with built-in underwear. I brought along a few pairs of shorts, some were longer, some shorter. When I had worn shorter pairs in the past, running through city streets as I sometimes did, I would hear strangers yell, "Run, Forrest, run!" Regardless, most of my shorts were starting to feel the effects of constant friction. Applying anti-chafing balm under my crotch and between my thighs was part of the daily routine and was as essential as any piece of my running attire. A layering system fluctuated on my upper body, depending on the weather and temperature. Most days, whatever layers were underneath, a plain blue cotton T-shirt with the words "Take Me Outside" printed on the front and "Run Across Canada" on the back was pulled over top. Mitts were temperature-dependent, as was the decision to wear a headband. On days like this one, both were needed as the snow fell hard on this late-March morning.

Amherst couldn't decide between winter and spring. An afternoon sun blushed the landscape with warmth, replacing the wet snow that had assailed me in the morning. Just as my clothes were beginning to dry out, dark clouds rolled in and snow pelted my bearded face from a strong crosswind. Crossing the border into New Brunswick seemed inconsequential. The landscape remained the same pale beige that marked the transition between those two seasons. Small hills that embanked either side of the Trans-Canada Highway opened into vast fields. Fields turned to forest where improbably skinny pines pricked the turbulent horizon.

To the south was one of the seven natural wonders of North America separating Nova Scotia and New Brunswick. Years earlier, I had experienced the Bay of Fundy, hiking Cape Chignecto with SP and our friend Matt. Carrying heavy backpacks and trudging up and down steep trails was the price of admission for the chance to view a dozen different species of whales and the highest tides found anywhere in the world.

Although it was tempting to veer off and head south to the bay, the TCH funnelled me northwest toward Moncton. Long, straight stretches of road like the one between Amherst and Moncton dulled my senses, allowing my mind to wander sporadically to thoughts of spaghetti and meatballs, what I would write that night and how long it might be before I could permanently exchange my winter running pants for shorts. I welcomed the clear mind, or perhaps a blank one, on these monotonous stretches. For years, running had been dual-purpose – it was often where I came to terms with the thoughts percolating in my head, sorting through the good and the bad. During the good, it was an opportunity to dissect life's obstacles, to deeply think about hard decisions. For the bad, it meant stewing about an unshakeable worry, beating out its tempo with each strike of my foot as I played its unsettling tune over and over in my head. Often, as was the case today, it was an opportunity to turn my brain off and to enter a meditative state that allowed me to lose myself in nothingness and boredom. It wasn't always a conscious decision as to which took precedence, the good or the bad, but rather an acceptance of whichever bubbled to the surface. After 37 kilometres of progress westward (and a beard full of wet snow), I retreated to the RV as the visibility on the highway was diminishing and the bluster of winter lived up to its east coast reputation. Moncton was only 24 kilometres away.

🍁

The Mi'kmaq and the Maliseet people were the original inhabitants of what we now know as New Brunswick. For thousands of years the land provided sustenance for its Indigenous occupants – they spear hunted large mammals like moose and caribou and harvested salmon from coastal waters, trapping them in stone corrals, scooping them up in loosely woven baskets and snaring them with bone hooks. Early European settlers relied on the Mi'kmaq for their survival upon contact, before forming governments and creating laws that decimated the culture of those who had lived harmoniously on the land for millennia. It's a familiar story across this country and an important story to be explored, one that is multi-faceted.

As a society, we are consumed with the notion of ownership, particularly the ownership of land. Award-winning novelist Thomas King alludes to this in *The Inconvenient Indian*, saying, "For non-Natives, land is primarily a commodity, something that has value for what you can take from it or what you can get for it… this is North America's societal attitude towards land." While he acknowledges that both sides, Indigenous and non-Indigenous, can differ from this generalization, there does seem to be an obsession over pieces of land that we consider "ours" – creating complicated documentation and long lists of rules in an attempt to make it official. Wars have been fought and millions have died over the right to own land. The soil, rock and water upon which non-Indigenous Peoples live and call "Canada" have certainly strained relationships with the first inhabitants of this land. But nor is it a singular issue. Whether it's government ownership, neighbours squabbling about a small patch of yard or families fighting over generational property, the importance of land ownership is deeply embedded in our psyche. It is difficult to break down the constructs built up over hundreds of years.

However, the land is unbiased – it is impervious to the idea of ownership. In fact, if the land could speak, it would likely reject the premise of ownership entirely. Some would argue that the land is already beginning to speak up with climate change showing the effects of how we try to own the land. The land needs us to be its guardians. This is the fundamental lesson of Indigenous Peoples. As King continues to say, "Land has always been a defining element in Aboriginal culture. Land contains the languages, the stories, and the histories of a people. It provides water, air, shelter and food. Land participates in the ceremonies and songs. And land is home. Not in an abstract way." As I ran, I was experiencing this land called Canada, not abstractly but tangibly – one planted step at a time. I could see the dawn of spring, and I could smell it. But perhaps, more importantly, I could feel spring awakening, both within my physical self and the landscape around me.

🍁

As I ran east, city centres became mere kilometre markers promising amenities. Moncton was no exception, as I basked in the warmth of a hot shower at the YMCA. Not showering had become the norm, more out of convenience than choice. It really didn't bother me as far as cleanliness went, although SP may have felt differently.

For me, the primary purpose of a shower on this journey had become warming up.

Another kind of warmth finally arrived. It was the end of March and the earth was finally tilting toward the sun rather than away. Halfway between Moncton and Fredericton, I was treated to the warmest day in two months. A visor replaced my winter headband, and the sun's rays closely pursued my progress most of the day. I found patches of dry grass on the side of the TCH where I paused to stretch and nibbled away on a roadside snack of nuts and chocolate. As I approached 41 kilometres that balmy afternoon, a white-tailed deer caught my attention off the highway inside some fencing. Wildlife fencing, a much-needed solution to curb the incidence of vehicle-animal collisions and the resulting fatalities, surrounded this particular stretch of the Trans-Canada. The deer was probably used to cars and trucks whizzing by, but it was startled by my six-foot-plus frame slowly approaching on the shoulder. The deer bolted, running west along the fence, rather than cutting back into the forest. It ran about 100 metres and then began grazing again on the grass at its feet. Less than a minute later, I caught up to it, startled it again and the deer loped away once more, running a little further west along the fencing. The cycle repeated itself numerous times before the deer finally scampered back into the cover of the forest, its namesake tail the last to disappear into the foliage. It reminded me of Christopher McDougall's book *Born to Run*, in which he describes how humans adapted to run long distances as hunters. Deer are faster than humans, but humans can run for longer distances than deer, tiring the animals out if tracked properly. I was happy to know this deer would live another day. Having a wildlife experience always feels special, whether it's seeing a beaver build its den in shallow waters, a moose lumbering its way through tall, grassy marsh or a deer grazing at the side of the busiest motorway in the country.

Powered by snacks and vitamin D, I soon put Moncton behind me. Three solid days had resulted in almost 135 kilometres of running. As I ran across the Princess Margaret Bridge into Fredericton, I smiled at the sight of people enjoying the day and the knowledge of a rest day in my immediate future. Running along the highway was a solitary experience, generally accounting for five or six hours every day. So, when two little kids peeled away from their mom on the sidewalk of the bridge and chased me for all of 20 seconds, I laughed and played along, feigning alarm at their pursuit. Is it intrinsic to want to catch someone moving quicker than you? To prove you can go fast too? It's not limited to kids either – over the years dozens of adults I have passed have also tried to keep up. Maybe Christopher McDougall was right that we are born to run – we just decide not to most of the time. Regardless, my pace, although pedestrian, still exceeded that of small children, so I continued running, knowing the end of the bridge was my finish line. Halfway across, I did a double take, looking back over my shoulder, realizing a wedding ceremony was underway. I wanted to yell congrats, but my introverted ways left me a silent observer. As my feet slapped out the final metres of the day's run, I reflected on the two significant life events happening simultaneously: a marriage ceremony and a 36-year-old attempting to run across Canada. How many other stories could the Saint John River tell?

We had scheduled two school visits for the next day. In the morning, we went to Nashwaaksis Middle School in north Fredericton. As we rotated through various grades and more than 700 students, two questions from students stood out: Do I know Justin Bieber? (I don't), and how exactly does being outside improve my self-confidence? Presentations were sometimes tough – engaging students in the conversation was paramount, but there was also an effort to share some of the emerging research. Even if the students zoned out, my hope was that the teachers would tune in. Research has shown that increased time outside can lead to better academic performance, better language skills, increased creativity and improved self-confidence. Again, research tends to focus on the *what* and the *how* and not always the *why*.

Admittedly, the answer I gave to the students, correlating my time outside to my own sense of self-confidence, seemed inadequate. It was a reminder of the disconnect that can sometimes exist when communicating peer-reviewed, evidence-based academic papers. Of course, research is informative and necessary, but reciting facts and statistics doesn't generally lead to changes in attitudes and behaviours. "Tell me and I'll forget; show me and I may remember; involve me and I'll understand." This Chinese proverb seemed an apt reminder that a shortcoming of the school visits was the small window of time I had to spend with the students. It was educators like Terry Kelly, a teacher at Devon Middle School in Fredericton, who were the difference makers – the teachers engaged with the students regularly, evoking change on a daily basis. The research is but a supporting tool.

🍁

Outside of the RV I was happy, conversational, upbeat and energized. But as soon as SP and I were in the Citation together, all of those good feelings were sapped, leaving a deflated shell. The weather was clearly unconcerned with our progress, as well as our mood – it was becoming perceptibly tough to be cooped up. Although I had pulled out my sandals after the run the previous day, it proceeded to snow 25 centimetres overnight. It was definitely taking a toll, but there was more to this increasing distance between us. I tried confronting the issue in a small and secluded parking lot we had found downtown behind a restaurant – our home for the night.

"Are you mad?" I asked SP.

"Nope."

"Can you tell me anything you're feeling?"

"I don't think so," she said firmly.

"I want to help fix it, but I need you to help me understand what I've done."

Her shoulders shrugged. I sighed loudly at this gesture.

"Can you please give me something?" I pleaded.

"No. It's fine," came the terse reply.

That word was so frustrating to hear. Everything was not *fine*. We were countless days and endless kilometres from *fine*. I was at a loss. SP didn't want to talk about it. She never wanted to talk about it. I didn't even know what *it* was. I was like a dog chasing its tail, running my mind futilely in circles, trying to pinpoint what mysterious ailment was causing the complete disintegration of civility within the plywood walls of the Citation. Years later, with the aid of perspective, I began to appreciate that there truly was no single cause of the friction but rather numerous factors that snowballed: cold, wet and smelly cramped quarters, finicky dogs, bum knees, a lemon of an RV, no plumbing, no money, lack of privacy – it was little surprise we didn't get along. But on that night in Fredericton I ran my fingers through my hair and growled in frustration. The next day, we coordinated our activities around spending as little time as possible in each other's space. I found comfort in walking Koona throughout the city and discovering warm places indoors away from the chill in the air and in the RV.

Koona loved winter. Bounding through untouched piles of snow, she would bury her head deep and pause, playing a game of hide-and-seek with herself. She took joy in rolling on her back, flailing back and forth, creating her own version of snow angels. As we wandered through parts of downtown Fredericton, we happened upon Odell Park. This 333-acre, year-round park is in the heart of the city where more than 16 kilometres of trails wind their way through an old-growth forest studded with 400-year-old inhabitants. That Saturday afternoon, a large group had gathered for a picnic amid the park's pond and playground. Their language was unfamiliar to me but didn't require translation; laughter, recognizable in any dialect, echoed throughout the park as kids threw snowballs, first at each other and then turned on their parents. I opened myself to the warmth and beauty of the Atlantic region, absorbing its spirit, willing it to seep into my being.

It was tough leaving Fredericton the next morning, but there was little choice but to keep moving west. Moments of freedom from the self-imposed obligation of running, or at least time off from what had come to feel like a job, perpetuated the emotional turmoil of getting back on the road. Spring returned yet again with a blue sky and a warm sun and within a few kilometres I was back on the Trans-Canada Highway headed for Edmundston.

New Brunswick is longer north to south than it is east to west, and the fact that my legs felt good meant I was making short work of this province. My face was starting to show the effects of longer days in the sun, freckles emerging as spring continued to advance. Days started to blur: Day 77 – 36.6 kilometres; Day 78 – 41.3 kilometres; Day 79 – 40.9 kilometres. My Garmin watch tracked every step and, although I paid minimal attention to it throughout the day, I was grateful to look down in the late afternoon and see progress. After another school visit to Woodstock Centennial, it was more of the same: Day 81 – 42.2 kilometres; Day 82 – 47.8 kilometres; Day 83 – 49.3 kilometres. The days were routine, yet each one held the promise of new experiences. For years, I had run the same routes over and over again, but for nine months and 7600 kilometres, I contemplated landscapes for the first time and watched the sun set on a different horizon each night.

🍁

One afternoon, as the highway veered north past Perth-Andover toward Edmundston, I noticed a dead coyote out of the corner of my eye. I had seen several dead animals over the past couple of months, the victims of speeding metal-and-steel machines. I stopped and was struck with emotion as I stared at the lifeless animal, thinking about its pure existence and the tragic end to it. Her head was draped over a rock exposed from the snow and ice that lined the ditch, just down from the shoulder of the highway. Her eye sockets were deep with darkness, crows having pecked out her eyeballs. Her mouth was agape, and dried blood was splattered across the dirty snow. Bits of hair surrounded her body, where scavengers had nibbled away at her. I couldn't help but feel a deep sadness. My species was responsible for the demise of the animal that lay battered at my feet. Coyotes are beautiful creatures, their yipping and howling often heard in the stillness of evenings. I told myself it was the cycle of life, but I was acutely aware of how weighted that cycle is in favour of my species. I began running again and, within minutes, my gait took me over a dead vole that had obviously been clipped by a car and died on the shoulder. I didn't break stride until I processed the harshness of my apathy a couple of kilometres further down the highway.

Why does the sight of a bear stir something greater inside of us than a raccoon? A warbler will almost always be more coveted in the eyes of birders over the common robin. A moose more than a red squirrel. A coyote more than a vole. Maybe it's how rare the species of animal is that guides our biases, but should that be an indicator of how much we value them? It irked me that I cared more for the coyote than I did for the vole. American naturalist E. O. Wilson says, "If all humankind were to disappear, the world would regenerate back to the rich state of equilibrium that existed ten thousand years ago. If insects were to vanish, the environment would collapse into chaos." It was only spring, but I sympathized with all the living creatures that would get squashed by windshields and grills in the coming months.

🍁

Saint Mary's Academy was the last school we visited in New Brunswick. A Grade 6 student shared with her peers and us her belief that people who lived their lives through the internet weren't living *real* lives. She vocalized the idea of a *fake* reality, one that is not based on real people and real situations. Much has been said on the topic of curated lives we see on social media. This student was getting at something even deeper, and I felt her words sink in. I was communicating with friends and family largely via email and only occasionally did I find time for meaningful conversations on the phone as well. It wasn't exactly a *fake* reality, but I felt empty. I was craving the physical presence of the people I cared about. I longed to look them in the eyes, to give my best friend a shot in the arm when he yanked my chain about something meaningless, or to receive a reassuring hug from my mother. I wanted to experience the nuanced gestures of their body language and feel them with me. People speak of finding a sense of community online, but I believe the deep connection that grows and strengthens relationships is absent online; it can only be achieved face-to-face. I appreciated the ability to keep in touch with those I cared about, but I yearned be in the same physical space as my friends and family.

On Day 86, I crossed the border into la belle province – Quebec – and the following day, I ran past the 2000-kilometre mark of our journey. It even snowed to commemorate my achievement. As I drew near to Rivière-du-Loup, a pretty town on the south shore of the St. Lawrence River, a cold wind tagged out the warm sun, and the mid-April day became reminiscent of winter. The penetrating chill was immediately forgotten as flashing lights pulled up beside me. It was the RCMP, and they peppered me with questions *en français*. I understood enough to glean they were asking if I owned the rickety RV parked ahead. After a fumbled response in French, they took pity on me and switched the conversation to English. I gave a quick summary of Take Me Outside and my attempt to run across Canada and was met with outstretched hands that I immediately interpreted as a friendly handshake. One of the officers handed me a business card and said the police would be happy to escort me along the Trans-Canada if needed. I chuckled as they drove away, picturing a cruiser following me at about seven kilometres an hour for six hours, thinking they might regret that offer. Regardless, it brought a smile to my face and I was grateful for the support.

🍁

The St. Lawrence River is young at heart, forming just 10,000 years ago when glaciers began retreating from the landscape of what is now southeastern Quebec. Originating in Lake Ontario, the river flows 1197 kilometres northeast toward the Atlantic Ocean, where it forms the Gulf of St. Lawrence. The entire St. Lawrence seaway, which encompasses the system of locks and channels permitting ocean-going vessels as far west as Minnesota, is more than 3000 kilometres in length from the gulf to the head of Lake Superior. In excess of 80 land and aquatic mammals and 400 species of birds call this river home, and it forms much of the southwestern border of the Canadian Shield.

Looking out over the farmland buttressing the St. Lawrence River, I was struck with its beauty, the smooth and levelled river accentuating the rolling hills sweeping their way up and down against the horizon. In time, I would discover how this land shaped humans far longer than I had been taught in middle school. Just as it's difficult to comprehend kilometre-thick ice covering any part of the planet for millions of years, let alone the St. Lawrence River and its surrounding valley, it's equally difficult to envision the nomadic people who began to inhabit this area 12,000 years ago. The Laurentide Ice Sheet, as it's known, covered the entirety of Quebec about 150,000 years ago. As the climate warmed and the ice melted, huge bodies of water formed. As thousands of years passed, land began to slowly emerge from the water, plants took root and animals appeared soon after. In time, nomadic people arrived on the unforgiving terrain, then comparable to barren tundra.

History is faithfully selective. Decades have been spent compiling documents and stories about European contact in this region considered to be the birth of our nation. Jacques Cartier arrived in the early 16th century and Samuel de Champlain in 1603, their names embedded in the Canadian conscience. Their stories play a prominent role in our history – even though Canadian Confederation didn't occur until 1867. But history is only factual in theory – it is told by the victors, so goes the familiar refrain, therefore it is fluid, interpretable. Historiography is uncovering the biases in our interpretation; the facts as they were presented throughout my school career are shifting. It is only recently that we have included Indigenous Peoples and the stories of the Iroquois who lived on the shores of the St. Lawrence 1,000 years ago; it is a familiar story, ignored by colonists the world over.

The history of Canada's story rarely includes the early Amerindian people of the Woodland period, who began to grow significantly in numbers 3,000 years ago along the shores of the St. Lawrence, adopting new practices like making clay pottery and growing corn. It was in this period that groups of hunter-gatherers travelled from the Great Lakes to settle in the St. Lawrence Valley. Seldom is there mention of the Archaic period, 6,000 years before the Woodland, and the adaptation of the Amerindian people to climate change as the ice retreated from the southern part of Quebec. The nomadic people of this era have only the remains of stone tools left of their story. Even less history is found in the Paleo-Indian period, where humans entered the St. Lawrence Valley 12,000 years ago as the kilometre-thick ice receded and the Champlain Sea began to shrink.

My feet pounded out a steady rhythm atop millions of years of slow, subtle shifts in geology along the St.

Lawrence. The modern world is categorized, sorted and filed by means of the constructs we have created – borders, governments and policies – with little consideration for the history of the people who lived symbiotically with the land for thousands of years.

🍁

The next day, flashing lights appeared again, and a different officer greeted me. I was informed this time that running or cycling was not allowed on the Trans-Canada Highway in Quebec. He mentioned a secondary highway that hugged the St. Lawrence River and ran parallel to the TCH, but I was devoted to this road and unsure about changing course. I had been navigating a love-hate relationship with the highway for months; I wasn't ready to give up on us. I asked if I could continue running until the next exit, to which he agreed. Driven by my devotion and the brief high of defiance, I decided to run through several more exits before calling it a day.

The very next day, flashing lights appeared for the final time. Yet another officer asked me, politely of course, to get into the back of his police car. I pled my case but to no avail – there was a firmness in his tone that I knew wouldn't budge. So into the back of the car I went, explaining that I needed to make sure he dropped me off on this other highway exactly in line with where he stopped me on the Trans-Canada. He obliged, and after a three-month commitment to the Trans-Canada Highway, we were forced to take a break. In that moment

I was angry – I felt the run was being compromised in some way. I was accustomed to the hum of the Trans-Canada's frequency and I had learned to affectionately tolerate its inadequacies. But, admittedly, I was pleasantly surprised by the peacefulness of Highway 132.

Winter still threatened to unleash its cold and snow, even though it was nearing the end of April. Blizzard-like conditions blew in north of Lévis and my mental fortitude was weakened. The RV rocked back and forth in the wind that night. We shivered inside, the consequence of giving up our search for propane. The *beep, beep, beep* of snowplows in the parking lot we called home that evening went on for hours. Koona had started to shed her winter coat and was now shivering as I tried to include her body in the mass of blankets that covered my cramped bed. I was connected to the weather in a way I never had been before, pushed and pulled along at its whim. It was a stark reminder of how humans have lived for thousands of years until we moved indoors permanently, electively out of touch with Earth's elements.

Forty-eight hours later, I basked in the blue sky and the bright sun as I ran, a warm spring breeze carrying my foul mood away with the dreary clouds. It helped that I turned northwest to cross over the St. Lawrence and began running on the north side of the river, headed toward Montreal, an indication that my time in Eastern Canada was diminishing.

It was Earth Day, and the correlation between

us and our relationship with the natural environment was heralded the world over. Rachel Carson's bestseller, *Silent Spring*, was published in 1962, raising public awareness about the environment, the organisms living in it and the clear and defining link between pollution and public health. In 1969, Gaylord Nelson was a US senator when a massive oil spill occurred in Santa Barbara, California. He pitched the idea for a "national teach-in on the environment," and with the help of Republican Congressman Pete McCloskey and 25-year-old Harvard student Denis Hayes, they put together events spanning the country. On April 22, 1970, 20 million Americans filled auditoriums and marched in the streets to demonstrate for environmental stewardship. Thousands of colleges and universities protested against the destructive relationship between humans and the environment. Earth Day in 1970 brought together Democrats and Republicans and led to a rare political victory: the creation of the United States Environmental Protection Agency and the passage of the Clean Air, Clean Water and Endangered Species acts. By 1990, Earth Day gained momentum and mobilized 200 million people in 141 countries, bringing environmental issues to the world stage. Today, Earth Day engages more than 75,000 global partners in almost 200 countries to address environmental issues. The power of millions coming together for a cause is powerful, yet an irony still existed for me: in a time when the natural environment needs us to get our act together, in our device-driven world, we are more disconnected than we've ever been.

❦

I hugged the river on Highway 138 heading southwest, small communities peppered the St. Lawrence and the land started to warm once more. As I started running southwest, north of Louiseville, Day 100 was upon us. I was adrift in time in our déjà-vu-type existence – Day 1 was still vividly alive in my conscience, yet in the jumble of peanut butter bagels and small towns I could have been convinced we were much further along.

 SP kindly bought a cake, candles and some champagne and planned to bike out to surprise me and celebrate the milestone, but our RV had other ideas. For the past two weeks, SP had run jumper cables from the auxiliary battery to the engine battery to fire up the beast. On that day, it not only needed the jumper cables but the generator as well. It took her an hour to get the RV going and, as a result, she didn't make it to me before I finished the day's earmarked kilometres. Although frustrated, she lit the candles, popped the cork, and I slipped my fork into some decadent chocolate cake.

"Well," SP said.

"Well," I replied, between bites.

"We survived 100 days," she said with a sly grin.

 I laughed but was unsure of her intentions in doing this – did she feel obligated to commemorate the moment, or was she genuinely happy that we had stuck it out for 100 days? I would never know but was grateful for the gesture. Chocolate cake made everything better and I found myself smiling ear to ear, proud of what we had both accomplished but also hoping, again, this might be a turning point in our temperamental relationship.

The next day was my sixth consecutive day of running. Strong winds, rain, sun and humidity challenged me physically. My legs were exhausted, but the reward for pushing through was the anticipation of two days off. By the end of the day, I had accumulated 270 kilometres over the six days, finishing in Repentigny, east of Montreal. We found Parc La Fontaine tucked in the centre of Montreal and parked, providing a much-needed break for the ailing RV, which seemed exhausted as well. SP had friends in the city and she quickly headed off for two nights in a bed that didn't require a feat of acrobatics to gain access to. For 48 hours, Koona and I lived the self-indulgent life of RV autonomy. Sleep had come easily over the last few months – I was typically in bed by 10 p.m. and would sleep until I naturally woke, which was usually around 8 a.m. Sleep was key to my recovery – enough rest enabled me to run marathon distances daily. That night there was extra satisfaction as I passed out, knowing that for the next couple of days my legs could be still.

As morning dawned, I lazed under the covers until Koona decided it was time to start the day. She had a park to explore – 84 acres of trails to walk, trees to sniff and endless patches of grass to mark her territory, which was beginning to add up, claiming a large swath of Eastern Canada. Originally, part of Parc La Fontaine was a farm until the government purchased it in 1845. Montreal bureaucrats had made a commitment to increase green space within the city and so a decision was made to create a public park. Ever since, amenities have been added, and the park has grown. By that afternoon, hundreds of Montrealers were chilled out on their own patch of former farmland. It was a spectacular day in the City of Saints – the park was full of people enjoying the fresh spring air.

The return to running was made easier by the outstanding weather, the catalyst for switching my running attire to shorts and a T-shirt. I was ecstatic to be done with layers. My friend Lilith joined me for seven kilometres as I made my way along Sherbrooke. It was fun to have a local tour guide as we ran past the Olympic Stadium, McGill University and the Musée national des beaux-arts du Québec. I reunited with the St. Lawrence River at the west end of Montreal by the end of the day, and my legs were refreshed rather than tired, allowing me to complete 48 kilometres. A radiant sunset painted the sky and capped off the day. SP and I shared some stories, but the conversation fizzled within minutes and the stillness in the RV drifted into the night.

The next day, I got some early miles in before SP picked me up for a school visit. College Bourget was a francophone school, but the English teacher had requested that I come speak with her Grade 10 students in English. Three hundred of them filled the auditorium, and immediately my words seemed lost in translation. I trudged through but was frustrated with my inability to speak enough French to smooth over my fragmented thoughts.

Afterward, a student came up and introduced himself. He asked me in his broken English how much passion it took to fuel my running.

"I want to run across Canada too," he said. "You have inspired me."

There was conviction in his face.

CHAPTER 5

A Hard Goodbye

Hugging the curves of the St. Lawrence River, I crossed from Quebec into Ontario on Day 106, according to the roadside boundary markers. During my nine months of running from coast to coast, those borders were extremely important to me – they marked progress and indicated achievement. They were tangible finish lines and the starting point for the next leg of my journey. Years later, I would read Kate Harris's book, *Lands of Lost Borders*, and begin to feel differently about the invented, intangible lines.

> We're so used to thinking of nations as self-evident, maps as trusted authorities, the boundaries veining them blue-blooded and sure. In places like Tibet, though, the land itself gives those lines the slip. Borders go bump in the night because they're reinforced by guardrails, but also because they exist in only suggestive, ghost-like ways. What if borders at their most basic are just desires written onto lands and lives, trying to foist permanence on the fact of flux?

Although Kate Harris wrote about her bike travels through the Silk Road in Tibet and beyond, her words seem fitting for Canada as well. Provinces and territories were slowly established over time, borders created to define them, with an ever-growing history of provincial divisiveness. And while political structures may be a necessity to govern large numbers of people, the land is blind to these borders. Can this nation find a more collective understanding of itself through the land, and the rivers, lakes and oceans, instead of imaginary lines penciled into maps?

For now, those maps and their veins of borders guided SP and me to the eastern edge of the notorious Highway 401, stretching more than 800 kilometres through Ontario, from the Quebec border to Windsor. Running on the 400 series of highways was not allowed, but, thankfully, my route was deviating to Ottawa before heading to Toronto. I had lived in Ontario for more years than I had any other province or territory, which brought comfort and ease to me as I ran among its familiar landscapes. The closeness of my friends beckoned and, for the first time in more than three weeks, I started to veer northwest, away from the St. Lawrence.

Like the land, the Citation was oblivious to borders and the new beginnings they supposedly heralded. SP spent another afternoon waiting for two flat tires to be fixed, while I battled fatigue through small, unassuming towns for the better part of 49 kilometres. It never occurred to us what role the RV would play in this journey – a constant thorn in the side of our progress.

The following day, jack pines, maple and birch gave

way to endless fields of corn. Barns were tucked behind farmers' houses lining the secondary highways. As I zigzagged my way on these smaller roads, I wondered how these communities would look in 50 years. I wondered about their stories – their history, the uncertainty of their future with younger generations continuing to shift to urban centres. Within these small rural communities, it's possible to track that change within a lifetime – the buildings and the people who inhabit them evolve. The land is no different, perhaps with the exception of time. It evolves, shifts and changes as well, but can take millions of years to do so. However, it seems we're more prone to seeing irregularities to the landscape with climate change escalating. Spending time outdoors – developing our relationship with the land – is one way we can help protect it. We need to find ways to reciprocate what the land offers us.

After 41 kilometres and another five straight days of running, my body was tired. I finished about 35 kilometres east of Ottawa, but because of numerous schools we were scheduled to visit, we drove into Ottawa. SP's mother was visiting from Halifax, and for most of the upcoming week she took a break from school visits, the RV and me. I'd visit nine schools in Ottawa before putting on my running shoes again. I met educators, health practitioners, government workers and parents; they welcomed me, fed me and supported the vision of Take Me Outside. That week in Ottawa was filled with engaging conversation and incredible people. Perhaps, not surprisingly, it continued to be my interactions with students that filled my bucket. If part of this journey was to inspire, inspiration was returned to me twofold. The students I met were thoughtful with their words and generous with their actions.

A running magazine had shown interest in our project and scheduled a photo shoot while we were in the Ottawa area. The sluggish pace I had adopted to enable my daily distances didn't quite capture the classic stride of a pure running form, so the photographer asked for some short sprints to achieve a more inspired image. I regretted my desire to please the camera that afternoon. Later, as I backtracked to where I had finished a week earlier and started my run into Ottawa, my calves and quads were screaming ten kilometres in from those quick sprints. Not having run for a week wasn't helping either. Every step was a struggle, as each kilometre seemed to draw itself out longer than the previous one. As I entered the city, however, and reached the Rideau Canal headed toward downtown, I was instantly stimulated by everything around me. Flowers were blooming, squirrels racing from one tree to the next and the pathway was full of runners, walkers and cyclists. My mind was renewed and, in turn, my body followed. My best friend, Dave, who was the first person I shared my dream of running across the country with, lived in Ottawa. He was meeting me on Parliament Hill, a place where we had shared numerous memories. I picked up my pace, eager to see his familiar face.

During university, Dave and I spent two summers with the Ceremonial Guard, stationed outside the residence of the Governor General in Ottawa. The changing of the guard and its accompanying band are a huge tourist draw on Parliament Hill during the summer months. The guard was composed of reservists and university students from across Canada. We were with the band; I played the trombone in the front row of the parade and Dave was a few rows back playing the euphonium. Each day we would march from the drill hall south of Laurier up Wellington in the heart of downtown Ottawa, our notes bouncing off the Chateau Laurier, a historic hotel overlooking the Ottawa River. The red wool tunics and massive bear hats we marched in were not ideally suited to the hot and humid summers in the Ottawa Valley. But even the oppressive heat could not stifle our patriotism as we paraded in unison onto Parliament Hill with bagpipers and foot soldiers in tow. On an average day, 5,000 tourists would surround the front lawn of Parliament Hill to take in the half-hour-long ceremony. Marches were played in slow and quick time, the Advance in Review Order performed and hundreds would gasp if a foot guard fainted, collapsing to the ground, a victim of stillness from the sun's intensity, to be carried off on a stretcher by nearby medical personnel. With time, this ceremony, the performance on the hill, became routine. However, the guard and the crowd always stood tall when we played "O Canada," our national anthem.

Canada's national anthem has a dizzying history, which is perhaps the reason it wasn't proclaimed as the official anthem until 1980, even though it was first performed at a banquet in the Pavillon des patineurs, in the City of Québec, in 1880. The original score, composed by Calixa Lavallée, still beckons us to rise at the beginning of NHL games, school assemblies and Remembrance Day ceremonies. The lyrics, however, have shifted over time. The original French lyrics, written by Adolphe-Basile Routhier in 1880, remain unchanged, but there have been numerous iterations of the English-language lyrics. Eventually, a poem written by Robert Stanley Weir was adopted in English-speaking Canada and, with the exception of a few minor changes, has remained to this day. The first stanza, the one that is recognizable as the national anthem, begins to speak to the vastness of our country: "From far and wide…" and the imagery of "The true north strong and free" gives way to feelings of civic pride. But it's Weir's second verse that really gives us a sense of the land:

> O Canada! Where pines and maples grow.
> Great prairies spread and lordly rivers flow.
> How dear to us thy broad domain,
> From East to Western sea.
> Thou land of hope for all who toil!
> Thou True North, strong and free!

Although the anthem conjured images of the red maple leaf rippling against the backdrop of a rich blue sky, the following day I ran in the rain. I loved it. Droplets of water fell gently from the murky sky and cooled my body as I ran out of the downtown core and toward Kanata. For some reason, I always enjoyed running in the elements, particularly when they weren't ideal: −40° Celsius, wind, rain, snow – it increased the challenge.

🍁

After a couple of more school visits, Day 120 marked four months of running toward the Pacific Ocean as I ran southwest through farmland, past sedentary cows chewing wads of grass. We had visited 34 schools and chatted with more than 14,000 students about spending less time in front of screens and more time outside. My legs had survived 2800 kilometres, the equivalent of 66 marathons. I ended the day with some cold-water immersion in one of the hundreds of small lakes that pepper the land between Ottawa and Peterborough. The water numbed my legs, but I knew the restorative qualities outweighed the temporary discomfort.

I met a middle-aged gentleman walking along the shoulder of Highway 7. He asked where I was running to and then spent the next 20 minutes foisting his opinions on me while I shuffled from foot to foot, anxious to keep moving.

"I hate technology. I hardly ever use it…" he started

in. "Kids these days..." He continued, trailing off as he watched wisps of clouds morph into familiar shapes above us.

"Food is key to running. You should be eating lots of vegetables and grains," he said, abruptly turning his attention back to me. "What are you drinking?" he demanded.

"Chocolate milk," I said.

"Chocolate milk?" he asked, incredulously. "You should only be drinking distilled water."

I thanked him for his time and strode off. I imagine he stood shaking his head, watching my shape grow small on the big horizon among the tall grass and farmed fields. He was one of countless people I met and had short conversations with as I ran across the country. Whether I spoke or listened, agreed or disagreed, these moments were a reminder of shifting the focus from the diversity that exists in this country and makes us different to what brings us together and can make us stronger. For me, the answer lies on the land we all stand on.

🍁

Over the May long weekend, SP escaped again, heading to Toronto to spend time with friends. So Koona and I found ourselves gloriously alone in the RV for the second time in two weeks. Talking to myself out loud was a practice I adopted in my late teens – I'm not exactly sure what prompted it, but it became my journal and my therapy rolled into one. While my daily runs on the TCH had allowed for this to continue, my evenings in the RV with SP were full of silence, so letting loose with my rambling thoughts out loud was a treat. The jaunt southwest from Ottawa to the Ontario peninsula felt short, and although it was tempting to push on, I welcomed the additional rest days. I was invited to stay at a friend's family cabin, located on a farm outside of Peterborough, so the RV sat empty for a few evenings. It was nice to connect with friends after the days of disconnect on the road, but I also relished the time alone. I had the opportunity to read through the dozens of letters we had received from students the previous couple of weeks. A smile began to take shape as the words of the students sunk in.

> Hi. I'm glad you came to our school and last night mainly I was playing outside until I had to get ready for bed.
> —Student

> Today you came to my school, and I just wanted to tell you how much I support and believe in what you are doing:) I think that the message you are trying to send to kids is a great one, and I agree that we should really spend more time in the great outdoors!:):) Since your presentation I have realized how important it is to stay healthy, and active and to enjoy outside. I will definitely try harder to be outside than to

stay inside and be on the computer 24/7! Thank you for making sure that this message is being sent to kids everywhere, and for sending the message to me!
—Student

When you run, do you look down at your feet or straight ahead?
—Student

I placed the last letter in my lap, sinking deeper into the couch. The notes from students had filled my heart, and inspired me to keep moving forward, but my legs were beginning to feel the inconsistency of starting and stopping. Rest days were important, but I was engaged in a pitched battle against inertia – I needed to get back on the road. More than two days off, and my body seemed to think it might be done with these daily long distances.

When I reacquainted myself with the highway shoulder and the surrounding cattle-flecked fields the next day, my right calf grumbled, letting me know that, if it had a choice in the matter, we would still be holed up at the cabin near Peterborough. We had numerous commitments up the road in Toronto, but I had left ample time to make my way there. I struggled to find the balance between appeasing an overworked body and too much rest.

🍁

In 2009, Christopher McDougall brought the fringe practice of barefoot running to the mainstream with his book *Born to Run*. From the seed McDougall planted, an industry of minimalist shoes grew, arguing we needed to get back to the roots of running. That is, the foot striking the ground in the mid-area, not the heel as is practically forced by the cushioned support of traditional running shoes. Over the past decade, and billions of consumer dollars, the shoe industry has flopped back and forth, pulling customers between glove-fitting shoes that have no cushioning to ones with sky-high platforms filled with foam. Not to mention a more recent marketing tactic by the industry that claims shoes should be changed out after 500 kilometres, a practice I knowledgeably protest. We lead ourselves to think that shoe companies have built the ideal shoe, until they come out with something even *better* the following spring. Trends shift and the cycle repeats as consumers search for that elusive perfect pair of runners.

Before I set off to cross Canada by foot, I tried and tried again to obtain a shoe sponsor, knowing the asphalt of the TCH would quickly eat up the soles and the structure of my most important piece of gear. Having been loyal to Saucony for almost two decades, I was reluctant to trust my feet to another brand. Nevertheless, numerous attempts to secure a few pairs of shoes from Saucony were unsuccessful, so I headed to Newfoundland, sponsorless, accompanied by a pair I had run in for half a year and another new pair that were untested. Running through the wet Maritime winter, I rotated between the two pairs daily, one always in the RV, waiting patiently for their turn on the asphalt. Eventually, the newbies became my favourite pair. There wasn't anything particularly special about the run-of-the-mill black trail runners, aside from the journey they were on, but each morning, when I slipped them on over my running socks and laced them up, they hugged my feet in all the right places. So devoted to these shoes was I, that after four months and almost 2500 kilometres the tread was flat, just a thin piece of foam, and the sides were full of holes, my big toe punching through to daylight with each footfall.

These shoes took me to the southern edge of Toronto along the lakeshore, which felt like a homecoming of sorts. Crossing over Keating Channel where the Don River empties into Lake Ontario, I was reminded of runs with my best friend Dave in Sunnybrook Park to the north. This watershed, one of the most urbanized rivers in Canada, stretches 38 kilometres from its headwaters in the Oak Ridges Moraine.

I was thrilled to see my parents, eagerly waiting at the edge of Lake Ontario near Sugar Beach later that afternoon. They had just returned from Windsor and Hamilton, a road trip to their hometowns to visit my aging grandmothers. We'd kept in touch via email and numerous phone calls, but this was the first time I'd seen them since leaving Winnipeg at the end of December for the east coast. In typical parent fashion, they beamed with pride as I approached; relieved as well to see I was alive and still running. Together, my parents and I ran the few short blocks to the base of Yonge Street to finish the day. SP was eager to split and catch up with friends, so I was able to speak candidly with my mom and dad over a steak and French fries on a patio in downtown Toronto.

"I wish I were happier at times during this," I said.

"That's fair," my mom responded. "But what you're doing isn't easy. And things that aren't easy don't always entail fun and happiness."

I spoke of the trials with SP, the concerns over money and how I was unsure if our meagre funds would allow us to finish our journey. And did they think I was having a lasting impact on the kids I met anyway? The presence of my mom and dad allowed me to let my guard down. For an evening, I became a kid in search of guidance, in need of the unwavering support of my cheering section. I soaked in every minute with them, grounded by virtue of their very presence.

The run was the actualization of a lifelong dream. Each step I took brought me one step closer to the Pacific Ocean. In many ways, I had become the best version of myself I could possibly be over the last few months: I was upbeat and energetic with students, had great conversations with teachers, I felt fitter than I ever had and I had the self-confidence that came with chasing a lifelong dream. It was confusing to feel pure joy in the tangible kilometres and yet feel the weight of uncertainty with the person who was with me day in and day out.

In the week to come, the doubts about whether this was all worthwhile faded to static, drowned out by new interest from media outlets in the Greater Toronto Area. I did interviews with CBC *Metro Morning*, Susan Hay on Global TV and an interview with the *Globe and Mail*. While I was grateful for some concentrated interest, it was still the students who kept pushing me west. Grade 7 students from Vimy Ridge Public School in Ajax sent me a short essay they had written, lauding the benefits of outdoor learning.

> Outdoor and Environmental Education (OEE) should be a separate subject taught in elementary school. OEE would provide an outdoor learning experience with physical and social health benefits. It would allow kids to connect to the earth and be physically active. The benefits are endless.
>
> OEE can help to improve the physical health of students. First, going outside to play and learn is physical exercise that will help kids maintain a healthy weight and reduce instances of childhood obesity. Secondly, learning and being active outside improves heart health. Thirdly, being active and outside at a young age will encourage children to remain active when they are older.

An OEE course would largely be hands-on. This would be beneficial as it would help those kinesthetic learners gain a better education. An OEE class at school would help kids gain an appreciation for the planet. This appreciation would likely lead to students making more environmentally responsible choices as a part of their lifestyle.

Students need a chance to explore and learn in the outdoors. They need a chance to connect with nature and be active. Adding outdoor education to the curriculum would do exactly that and more.

The 12- and 13-year-olds concluded their essay stating OEE improves the social and emotional health of students, allowing them to showcase their strengths in a way not possible in the classroom. They also argued that it requires teamwork and builds character, both factors in increased confidence and mutual respect. Months later, after dipping my toes into the Pacific and settling into Victoria, I had the opportunity to interview the future prime minister, Justin Trudeau. Knowing that teaching was in his past, I thought he might be able to share some thoughts that would help spread the Take Me Outside message. I was pleasantly surprised when he agreed to my request. Trudeau reiterated the sentiments of the Grade 7 students, though perhaps not as eloquently:

> We have to recognize that all students learn differently. It's wonderful that we're bringing more computers and virtual learning into the classroom and tweaking the way we do things... but I think it's also an opportunity to counterbalance that by saying: "OK, if we're going to bring in more technology we also have to get them to come outside more often." If we properly start getting them away from the desk, we're going to be able to be much more effective in how we raise young Canadians.

❦

Ten days after arriving in Toronto, I hit the road again, this time on busy Yonge Street. I was replenished from interacting with so many students and teachers, and hopeful that this would fuel me as I found myself oriented due north. I needed every bit of motivation I could muster heading off the densely populated Ontario peninsula and tracking along the northern edge of the Great Lakes en route to Western Canada.

On Day 154, I ran from south of Barrie, almost all the way to Orillia, hugging Lake Simcoe to the east. We had been in Ontario for more than six weeks, and I had only managed 600 kilometres, a distance I would have typically knocked off in half the time. However, a more significant feat during these weeks was 36 school visits. Despite the warm welcomes and slew of letters, I often found myself second-guessing the impact of the Take

Me Outside assemblies and presentations. In an age of analytics and metrics, do one's convictions still matter if they don't add up to something tangible?

With the end of the school year just days away, my focus swung from in-school meet-and-greets back to running; I needed to put in solid days this summer to avoid running through the beginning of winter in the Rockies. I acquainted myself with the pace of cars and trucks speeding north as I rejoined Highway 11 nearing Orillia, and accepted that my slow stride was a necessity to preserve my IT band after weeks of inconsistent running.

Just as the running had been sporadic for those six weeks, so too was the time SP and I spent together in the RV. Southern Ontario had been brimming with friends and social engagements, and the cyclical nature of our time there made the moments in each other's company tolerable: a short stint together and then a break, a chance to recharge. There were no fights during these days back together, and although conversation was always scarce, our mood generally remained pleasant, knowing that the next break was never far away. However, as we left Toronto and headed north, there was a distinct shift in SP's demeanour, made obvious by her clipped conversation and tone.

"You want to talk about anything?" I asked.

"Nope."

Sammy and Koona must have sensed the silence that permeated the RV that night as not another word was spoken. We exchanged a bare minimum of words the morning of our 155th day. My IT band loudly protested the plotted 42 kilometres, forcing me to walk. For seven and a half hours, I ruminated on the details of RV life, chewed on them, attempting to discern fact from overtired, cramped, smelly fiction. That evening resounding silence returned to the Citation.

The next day, my IT band started to feel a little better, and I was able to throw in short spurts of running, but it was still a day dominated by walking along Highway 11. Over lunch, SP disappeared from the RV without saying a word, the door squeaking shut behind her more forcefully than usual. I sat eating my turkey sandwich, feeling the increasing weight of silence and discomfort with what was happening. She didn't return before I headed back out for the afternoon, which meant she didn't know where to pick me up at day's end. Even though the routine of 20 to 25 kilometres was indeed routine, there was always a check-in just in case. That afternoon, as I walked and ran north of Bracebridge, I reached a tipping point. As I walked through scenarios over and over again on Highway 11, I was convinced that something had to give. My racing thoughts eventually stilled, leaving one solution; I rehearsed what I would say when we eventually met up that evening down the road. Thirty-five kilometres later, the hulking silhouette of the RV appeared on the horizon. SP picked me up and we headed back to Bracebridge, in Ontario's fabled Muskoka region.

"Hey, can we chat?" I asked.

"Sure," she said hesitantly.

"I'm at a loss. I don't know if you're mad at me, or upset with something else, but something is wrong and it's weighing on me. And I'm guessing it's weighing on you."

I have a tendency to ramble when I think someone else is at a loss for words. So, true to form, I kept talking. I acknowledged how hard the journey had been for us, what an impossibly long five months we had endured. I told her how grateful I was that she had forfeited almost half a year to be the sole member of my support crew. I thanked her for the cooking, for all the crappy jobs that were dumped on her – the litany of RV issues, the finicky generator, exercising the dogs – I rambled on and on, unsure when I had said enough. On the verge of tears, I arrived at the crux of my ramble – it felt impossible to spit out what I had practised numerous times alone on the highway.

"I think I should drive you to Toronto so you can fly home to Halifax," I said eventually.

"OK," she responded.

For a moment, I was surprised. I thought she might put up a fight to stay, if for no other reason than to disagree with my suggestion. She softened immediately, and her tone was genuine.

"I feel like I'm letting you down," she said. "I don't want to leave you hanging, but I think this is what I need."

Peace settled over the RV. All of the tension and the difficult silences disappeared and for a moment it felt like we were friends again.

"What are you going to do?" she asked.

"I don't know, but I'll figure it out."

Serenity often accompanies embracing the obvious. We had tried, and now we were at the end, the once-palpable anger and frustration dissolved with the passing kilometres as we headed south to Toronto.

The sudden departure of SP would have a massive logistical impact on my daily movements. She had committed to join me for seven months, allowing her to return to Halifax to teach in September. Neither of us predicted the run through Newfoundland would take as long as it did, that there would be a growing number of school visits or that I would be wracked with injury – those factors all combined to knock us so far off schedule that the predetermined seven months to cross the country seemed preposterous. I didn't have a replacement lined up to fill SP's shoes, and that was concerning. But it still felt like the right decision.

Early that evening, we pulled into the driveway at her friend's house in Toronto, and together we piled all her belongings on the lawn: her bedding, her books, clothes, her bike and, of course, Sammy.

"I guess you won't need the baby gate anymore," she said with a smile.

"Ha! I guess not." I said. "I don't know how to say thank you for everything you've done."

"It's all good," she responded. "You can do this."

We hugged and she waved goodbye as I backed the RV out of the driveway. I didn't know it would be one of the last times we spoke.

CHAPTER 6

Alone

After parting ways with SP, I drove north toward Hunstville to a new beginning. There were many *firsts* that afternoon. Koona was lying in between the driver and passenger seats – the first time she had been in the front of the RV. I wondered if Koona was missing Sammy for the first time. Having started out mortal enemies in a confined space, the dogs eventually became apathetic toward one another's existence. For the first time, I assumed the role of chauffeur and chef – boiler of water, maker of ten-minute dinners. My emotions were all over the map. For the first time in five months, SP was not there helping me, supporting me, talking to me, not talking to me or listening to me. On the one hand, I was gutted. Maybe I wasn't grateful enough. Maybe I was too focused on the running and blogging and school visits and didn't give the friendship the attention it deserved. *Did I mess this up? Was it my fault she left?* On the other hand, I was relieved. RV life had become unbearable and although finger pointing was tempting, we were both to blame.

I enjoyed being alone, as introverts do. I was excited by the prospect of talking to myself out loud in the RV and not having to consider another human; the needs and wants of Koona were relatively simple. It was the right decision and I knew SP agreed, even though it was hard for either of us to admit. It could not be understated: five months in that RV together, three of which were winter, had been extremely difficult. Given the healing power of time, some time apart, I was confident we would sort it out as we always had so often in the past.

The road ahead troubled me. Summer was just starting, friends and family had plans for the short Canadian season and they didn't include driving a decrepit RV through central and Northern Ontario in 50-kilometre increments. My dad offered to help, but he couldn't join me until the beginning of August. The choices were clear: either find a way to do it on my own, or put the journey on hold until I could find a willing participant to drive support. The decision was easy. I had come so far – I was almost halfway across the geographical expanse of Canada, more than 3000 kilometres were behind me, 156 days. Quitting was not truly an option. As I dug in my heels, I formulated a plan that would allow me to continue.

I had a bit of experience hitchhiking. Admittedly, not all positive, but without a dedicated driver I couldn't see another option. For the next five weeks I woke, took Koona outside, gobbled down my usual breakfast, then drove north for 25 kilometres. From where I parked, I would hitchhike back to where I'd finished the day before and run to the Citation and Koona, all before lunch. At midday, I'd have lunch, exercise Koona, then run another 25 kilometres and thumb a ride back to my patiently waiting best friend.

Variations of this would present themselves in the coming weeks, but at the time it was the best plan I could envision. One of my top concerns was Koona. I wasn't overly concerned about the summer heat – the RV stayed cool, even in hot weather. And I wasn't too worried about being gone for six hours a day – she was used to time alone from our days in Haliburton. But I was about to travel through a remote stretch of Northern Ontario with fewer pit stops than any other province. It could be pretty remote along the TCH, even in these summer months, and although breaking into a beat-up RV seemed unlikely, it was still a possibility.

I adopted a one-day-at-a-time approach. I started packing a midday meal and plenty of snacks. I had used a hydration pack consistently, but ensuring the pack was full with three litres of water was imperative unless I knew I was going to hit a lake. Lake Superior would be beside me eventually but not always accessible, and certainly not for the next couple of weeks.

After driving back up north from Toronto, I parked the RV at a Walmart just outside of Huntsville and tracked back to the highway to catch my first ride back south to my starting point. I stuck out my thumb and Tom picked me up. He lived in the Huntsville area and his life story spilled out of him within our first five minutes together without so much as taking a breath. For the subsequent 15 minutes, Tom presented a well-rehearsed discourse on the Holy Trinity. I considered telling him my parents were ministers and that I was well versed in the story of the Father, the Son and the Holy Ghost, but instead I listened quietly, astonished by his ability to speak continuously without stopping for air. I quietly pointed to where I needed him to stop and even as the car came to rest on the shoulder, he continued his mission to convert me. Then, surprisingly, he stopped talking long enough to inquire why I wanted to get out at a nondescript spot on the highway. I told him I was running across Canada, which caused him to launch into another tale, this one about his plan to walk across Canada carrying a cross, just like Jesus did on the day of his crucifixion. I hastily exited the Hummer and started running. It was going to be an interesting few weeks.

Since starting this journey, I had heard regularly from friends and family via email, text and the occasional phone call. The most common words of encouragement I received were "one day at a time." However, putting the refrain into practice was immensely more difficult than merely uttering the words, or even believing it for that matter. I had spent the majority of Newfoundland overwhelmed by the big picture, thinking constantly about the unknown road ahead. It took a concerted effort to focus on the day at hand. Incremental finish lines were necessary, and more so in Northern Ontario where I played the exhausting game of RV leapfrog for weeks. The logistics of each day looked different with SP not there, and the routines I had become accustomed to were adjusted. But *one day at a time* was the only option to keep moving forward.

Day 158 – 26.6 km
Day 159 – 34.7 km
Day 160 – Rest
Day 161 – 42.1 km
Day 162 – 30.7 km

At the end of Day 162, I found a beach in North Bay, a city that saw little activity until the arrival of the Canadian Pacific Railway in 1882. I looked out over Lake Nipissing as Koona rolled in the short grass, both of us soaking in the sun. Only seagulls frolicking above interrupted the quiet depth of the blue sky. Small waves lapped the sandy beach and my mind wandered to the eclectic assortment of people who had offered me rides: a hobby farmer, a mechanic, a mining engineer from Iran and a pot dealer.

The next day, as I ran out of North Bay, I headed west again instead of north, which felt good mentally. Physically, I was in rough shape. My left knee continued to nag me, and when I peeled off my running sock at the end of the day, it revealed a golf-ball-sized blister on my left heel and another dime-sized one on my baby toe.

Years earlier, I had adopted a mid-foot strike to my running stride – landing on the balls of each foot. A groundswell of research convinced me the muscular-skeletal system of humans evolved amid barefoot running. It seemed to make sense: removing shoes to run in the grass would result in most people naturally landing mid-foot – it was just too painful to land on the heel. But with the advent of running shoes, along with our increased tendency to live in concrete cities, the natural form of a mid-foot strike slowly shifted to take advantage of the cushioned heel. So, although a lot of runners still plant their heel first, there are a growing number of runners switching back to the natural barefoot stride. I was one of them. Walking, however, still forced a heel strike, and I was fairly certain the rubbing caused by the mechanics of walking caused the blisters, not the running. Regardless, my body was readjusting to consistent movement after weeks of start-stop in Southern Ontario – pressing on was crucial to my momentum. Although the blisters were hideous to look at, once wrapped the next day, they didn't bother me.

🍁

On Canada Day, I needed to make forward progress, but my heart wasn't in it. After 18.5 kilometres, and the heat of the sun getting more intense, I decided to celebrate the day with Koona with some extra walks and by taking in some of the festivities local to Sudburians. I had run through several provinces that would collectively be having their own festivities this day. Across the country, there were citizen ceremonies, welcoming new Canadians. However, I had also run through treaty land – land that had been occupied for thousands of years. Many First Nations, Inuit and Metis people would not celebrate this day that focused on Confederation. I was torn and unsure of how to celebrate this country I felt fortunate to live in. Perhaps, in a time of reconciliation, there's an opportunity to turn our attention more toward what we all have in common – the land we live on. Could celebrating Canada Day give less attention to an "anniversary year" that seems to divide us and focus more on what unites us – the land and how it shapes our nation?

The humidity of an Ontario summer has a stifling presence, like a cloak you can't shrug off. I ritually lathered myself in sunscreen only to have it slide off my skin in the heavy, wet air.

Day 163 – 41.5 km
Day 164 – 42.2 km
Day 165 – 18.6 km
Day 166 – Rest
Day 167 – 36.1 km

Over the course of four days, 138 kilometres and eight thumbed rides, I arrived east of Sudbury, exhausted and sunburned. Eager to see Lake Superior, I tried to remain mentally strong, which meant continuing on without a day off. I ran past Whitefish, Espanola, Webbwood and Spanish. The shoulder of the Trans-Canada became monotonous. The adventure and promise of new experiences took a back seat to effort and progress. Head down, I willed my legs on: *One more kilometre. Just to the top of the hill.* I began to care less about making eye contact with drivers – it was too much effort. When I did look up, an audience of trees, marsh and Canadian Shield quietly cheered me along. In the span of three days, I ran 121 kilometres, putting in more than 15 hours of running and an additional few hours of hitchhiking. I tried my best to ignore the fact that my three-day achievement would take just over an hour by car.

In Algoma Mills, east of Blind River, I walked the short distance from the RV to the highway and assumed the universally accepted hitchhiking gesture of one arm extended, thumb up. So far, I hadn't waited more than an hour for a ride. I must not have looked like a potential threat in running attire, or people really do crave human interaction.

Traffic was quiet that morning, but with the confidence of numerous rides under my belt, I tried not to fret as the first hour passed. I was frustrated the day was off to such a slow start, but I countered that by acknowledging my good fortune thus far. In the second hour, I tried various tactics: I smiled the biggest, most disarming smile I could muster, I stood up straighter – good posture, good morals – I made more eye contact. When those efforts didn't yield a ride, I walked a dozen metres, hoping a change in location would bring me luck.

As the clock crept past hour two, I wondered if something was wrong. *Was this the Bermuda Triangle of hitchhiking? Was I in the dark about a hitchhiking incident in this area?* I began talking to myself out loud between the cars that whizzed by at fairly regular intervals – *was I invisible?* I looked down at my hands, touching one against the other. Still there. I scanned every vehicle that passed, most had ample room for an additional passenger, albeit a stranger. Was some sort of Morse code being relayed from one driver to the next to avoid the bearded ginger on the side of the Trans-Canada? Although it was summertime, this area was a thoroughfare, not a destination, and no one stopped.

After three hours of waiting, I resorted to a game I had played as a teenager while nervously waiting for a phone call from a crush. I would count down from ten, positive the phone would ring before hitting zero. I did the same that morning, counting down the number of cars that passed from ten, convinced a car would pick me up before counting the tenth car. Again, just as in my teen years, the game failed me. I was restless, frustrated and angry. I had 33 kilometres to run and had been standing still for more than three hours. It was like getting to the start line of a race three hours before it started. I thought about walking back to the RV, driving to my start point and then hoping for a change of luck trying to hitch a ride back. But the RV was in a great spot for Koona, and there was still a thread of hope that someone would stop soon. So I waited a fourth hour and as it came and went I was truly at my wit's end. I couldn't wait any longer. For the first time in nearly six months, I ran east. I momentarily questioned my decision, but my rationale was sound: regardless of whether my start to finish line entailed running east to west or west to east, I was still running across Canada. On this day, I just happened to be heading a different direction than I had been for months.

Hours later, I arrived at my start point, which had become my finish line. My self-confidence was low, and it was with trepidation that I stuck out my thumb to hitch back to Algoma Mills. Exhausted, I was eager to get back to Koona and be done with the day. Within half an hour, a truck stopped and a man named Mike opened the passenger door and asked where I was headed. I looked into the empty back seat and saw some toys and a stove. Mike was on his way to Thunder Bay to visit his kids and take them camping for the weekend. Too tired to initiate conversation, I was thankful Mike was friendly and happily carried the conversation for the 20-minute ride. He, of course, asked what I was doing on that uninhabited stretch of highway, and I gave him the Take Me Outside summary. Mike then talked to me about the concerns the area Elders had about the environment. As an Indigenous man himself, he feared the impacts some forestry practices and humans were having on wildlife. When he dropped me off, he handed me a generous donation and imparted some powerful parting words: "Keep your ears open to everything that you will encounter on this journey – the trees, the animals, the wind. You are on a special journey."

The next few days were distinguishable from one

another solely by the names of the towns I passed through.

Algoma Mills to Iron Bridge – 38.5 km
Iron Bridge to Bruce Mines – 46.3 km
Bruce Mines to Desbarats – 11.8 km
Desbarats to Sault Ste. Marie – 46.1 km

When I reached "the Sault," Sault Ste. Marie to the unacquainted, my desire to touch the water – to feel the essence of Lake Superior – superseded my craving for the amenities of a city, so again, I decided to carry on. After another day and another marathon distance, I arrived at Harmony Beach and finally saw Superior in its fullness from shore – a blue abyss stretching to the horizon.

🍁

Human obsession with the biggest, the fastest and the strongest doesn't exclude our natural conquests. We're fascinated with Everest being the highest mountain, the Amazon being the longest river and, here in our backyard, Lake Superior – the largest freshwater lake (by surface area) in the world. So massive and deep is this lake, it could cover the entirety of North and South America with a foot of water. Its fog and harsh winds have claimed more than 1,000 lives, and it has sunk more than 350 ships, battered by wave and wind, too far from help in the vast inland ocean. Gordon Lightfoot told the tale of the SS *Edmund Fitzgerald*, the namesake freighter that sunk in 1975, killing all 29 on board. Lake

Superior was a pivotal location for the Group of Seven painters, with its rugged and rocky landscape on the northern shores. Lawren Harris, one of the seven, had several paintings of Superior that were the highlight of actor Steve Martin's curated show that toured North America in 2016. Harris proclaimed the breathtaking landscape "existed nowhere else in Canada." Perhaps a bold statement, but one that so many artists might exclaim of the beauty in their own parts of the country.

Years earlier, when I lived in Haliburton, evenings were social – there were no clubs or bars, at least none my friends and I gravitated toward. Instead, we enjoyed the coziness of a cabin, telling exaggerated stories ad nauseam for a laugh. Once every few months, someone would put Bill Mason's *Waterwalker* on the TV late into the night and we would be mesmerized by the draw of the paddle along the Superior shores, eased by the music of Bruce Cockburn that accompanied this feature-length film.

🍁

The following day, the highway began to truly hug the shores of Lake Superior. I tried to stay alert as vehicles sped by on my right. Thirty-nine kilometres didn't exactly fly by, but I was pleasantly distracted by pebbled beaches and rocky inlets. When I arrived at Pancake Bay Provincial Park five hours later, the day's finish line, I was happy to sit on a sandy beach and give the waves my full attention. Cell coverage had disappeared somewhere north of the Sault, and I was relieved to not have to answer texts or phone calls or emails or write another blog. The sky turned shades of pink and purple from the orange sun, a glowing orb disappearing into the shimmering waters of the lake. I sat, enwrapped in solitude.

The next morning, I imagined I was heading out for a morning jog. Walking from the RV to highway, I was relaxed and thankful I didn't have to start my day thumbing a ride, as my start line was the entrance to the campground. Again, the lake riveted me as I ran; rays of hot summer sun caught the tips of small waves and sparkled like the night sky. I had plotted a shorter run than usual that day, and soon I was at the southern edge of Lake Superior Provincial Park. After a short ride back to Pancake Bay to retrieve Koona and the RV, we drove into the park and found a campsite along the water's edge in Agawa Bay. We arrived in the early afternoon, so time was plentiful. After four days of decent distances, I had decided to take the next day off. I revelled in the moment, a long summer day stretched out before us with nothing to do and nowhere to be. A lazy afternoon blended seamlessly into a lazy evening. I built a fire, Koona sprawled at my feet, and became mesmerized by the embers cracking and popping from the firepit, a metal cauldron sunk into the earth.

After a long sleep, I awoke to the sound of other campers beginning their daily routines, the smell of bacon wafting over to me as I prepared my predictable toasted bagel with peanut butter. Koona signalled it was time to start the day, her downward dog pose accompanied by her vocal yawn. As we wandered through the campground, I envied the people settled in for a lengthy stint of relaxation. I had but one free day, and although I intended to explore and make the most of it, we stuck close to the campsite, content to lounge about.

It was difficult to leave such a beautiful spot after only one day off. I tried to block out visions of lounging by the lake with Koona, throwing small rocks from the shore with a warm wind blowing in from the lake. It took less than half an hour to hitch a ride south to then retrace the distance back to the campground. It was slow going as I started running north, but I was steadfast in my resolve to arrive back at the Agawa Bay campground to enjoy as much of the afternoon off my feet as I could.

There were long stints with no traffic, and the rhythmic beat of my shoes on the shoulder was the metronome for a consistent pace. For the most part, I never ran with headphones – during the last six months or previous to that. There were some exceptions, particularly on the days where walking had been necessary. When I ran, I preferred to be immersed in the surrounding environment. Also I was in bear country, and my senses were heightened when cars were absent. After 34.9 kilometres, I arrived back at Agawa Bay to find Koona fast asleep on the cool linoleum floor of the RV. The afternoon slipped into evening quicker than I hoped. I built another fire and settled into my camping chair, eager for the flames to clear my mind as they had the night before. But as I sat alone in front of the crackling fire, I felt lonely. Laughter from the adjacent campsites echoed through the tall pines and I longed for a friend to share my thoughts with, to share the beauty of the summer evening.

I awoke the next morning to the sound of waves gently lapping the shore of Lake Superior. Any sense of loneliness had slipped away into the infinite night sky. I imagined spending a week at this campground on the lakeshore in uninterrupted solitude, deepening my relationship with its environment. I had minimal desire to put on running shoes, and even less desire to break into a running stride only to have sunscreen slowly sweat its way into my eyes. I caught myself procrastinating as I swept out the sand and dirt from the entrance of the RV – I knew the work part of my day needed to begin. Even though there were no school commitments or media to chat with, running across the country was still integral to establishing Take Me Outside and its message. The dream of this cross-Canada journey had become a job of sorts, but what dream doesn't require work in order for it to come to fruition? Incentives were paramount – once I ran the day's marathon, I would return to the campground for one last coveted evening before shuttling forward to a new location. I had been fortunate to be based out of that blissful space for a few days, which made it harder to come to terms with my time there ending.

As I walked out to the highway, adjusting the full water bladder against my back, I hoped it would be an easy day. Thankfully, my starting point was at the turnoff for the campground, which meant I could simply start running north. Within the first kilometre, I was already anticipating the soothing cool water of the lake that would greet my body once finished. A pedestrian stride took me 42.8 kilometres in five hours and 45 minutes, according to my watch, but my time was of no consequence. The only proof needed for this journey was that I had covered the distance in a growing collection of entries on the Garmin website, showing bit by bit my progress across the country. The following day was even slower, having to walk significant stretches because of the pain that was still nagging my left knee. After 43.3 kilometres, exhaustion set in, exacerbated by the energy-sapping blanket of humidity that lingered near the lake. I waited three and a half hours for a ride that day – my eyes welling with tears, stuck in the remoteness of Ontario's hinterland. The following day, my legs felt better, my knee stronger and 40.2 kilometres took considerably less time – my spirits lifted. It helped that I was picked up within 15 minutes.

🍁

If I needed any assurance that journeys, like the one I found myself on, are born of conviction, proof was delivered to me on that remote stretch of Ontario highway. Having completed a 51-kilometre day, which put me in

White River, Ontario, I was grabbing an early dinner at a gas station restaurant when I overheard a small group of cyclists telling stories about their respective cross-Canada journeys. It was prime biking season – the time of year when those so inclined made cross-country treks by bike, typically going west to east to take advantage of favourable winds. Starved for social interaction, I overcame my introversion and asked if I could join their conversation. I was eager to interact with people experiencing a journey by bike, a welcome change from the brief exchanges of my thumbed rides. Erik, Annik and Corrine were biking from Winnipeg to Newfoundland to raise money for cancer research. Sam was from Kamloops and was cycling for women's freedom in Nepal. Nikki was cycling east to west, raising money for Free the Children, an organization dedicated to youth empowerment and international development. It was inspiring to sit and listen to their stories. We laughed as we swapped tales from the road, sharing legendary feats of carb-loading and drivers who thought they were being funny by veering closer to the shoulder as they approached. The next morning, two cyclists stopped me on the highway shoulder. Nikki, who had an earlier start than I, had shared my story with them and in return I heard theirs briefly – a young couple from BC who were riding for Doctors for Doctors, a nonprofit focused on increasing access to healthcare internationally. More kindred spirits. It was, however, a chance encounter the next day that would have the greatest impact.

On Day 187, I was just east of White Lake Provincial Park, close to finishing my day, my mind wandering to the calm lake beckoning my tired legs, when I saw him walking east toward me. As we drew closer to each other, he crossed the highway and I saw his name printed on the side of the buggy he pushed. It was Jean Béliveau (not the Jean Béliveau of hockey fame, who played 21 seasons with the Montreal Canadiens). This Jean Béliveau had been walking around the world for the past 11 years, travelling more than 75,000 kilometres. Having done my homework on other solo journeys wandering the Trans-Canada that summer, I knew he was on his last stretch of his journey from Vancouver to Montreal, and that he had dedicated his journey to promoting peace and awareness for children facing violence in their daily lives.

An extra pair of running shoes was strapped to the top of his oversized buggy with bungee cords. A plastic bag hung off the handles and a sun hat and raincoat were the cherry on top of the piecemeal assemblage. Jean's smile was the first thing I noticed, even before his greying hair, wire-rimmed glasses and the blue bandana tied loosely around his neck. The energy in his voice was emphatic as he showed me his scrapbook filled with pictures of mountains and hillsides, cities and people who had welcomed him, deserts and vast expanses of landscapes that only he could pinpoint. He had likely told his story to thousands of people over the years, but the enthusiasm with which he shared his story did not waver. It was surreal to stand next to this man in the middle-of-nowhere, Northern Ontario, hardly a car to be found.

Jean's humour and smile struck me, but it was his humility that astounded me. He had garnered worldwide attention for his efforts, but as we stood together on the side of the highway, he was just another human living out his convictions. They had fuelled him to make this a meaningful journey. If this man's convictions had carried him around the world for 11 years, I hoped that mine would push me west to the Pacific Ocean for another three months. At the end of our 20-minute conversation, I extended my arm to shake hands. He obliged but then asked if he could give me a hug. He squeezed me tight, and all I could do was cross my fingers and hope his uplifting spirit would accompany me for the rest of my journey.

That evening, I felt energized. And happy. As darkness set in over White Lake, I replayed our conversation over and over, hoping his words would soak deep within me.

The next day, the high of meeting Jean was quickly quashed by the task at hand. After four kilometres, pain and fatigue resurfaced and I thought I might have to walk the rest of the day. I tried to will Jean's enthusiasm into my tired body, and for a while it worked. I put my head down and slogged out 30 hard kilometres into the afternoon. My finish line was the town of Marathon, and it seemed only appropriate to try and complete the equivalent distance that day. A few hundred metres past the town's exit, I clocked 42.2 kilometres, the marathon distance. I had run for eight days straight, covering 304 kilometres.

❦

I had grown unmotivated by my daily finish lines, so instead I slipped into contemplating the dizzying amount of blacktop that lay ahead. While I ran, I habitually rearranged the kilometres in my mind, adding and subtracting, trying to arrange the numbers in a palatable fashion: another 306 kilometres to Thunder Bay, and then 800 kilometres to the border of Manitoba. Since crossing from Quebec into Ontario, I had run more than 1700 kilometres. Exiting Ontario would mean I had run 2500 kilometres across the province, one-third of the distance for the entire cross-country run. After Ontario, 2500 kilometres still remained.

I had arranged for my dad to join me in early August to fill the vacant role of team support. I was eager for his help, but I craved the comfort of his embrace more. I felt like a little kid in need of assurance and longed to hear him say, "Everything's going to be just fine, son." Time ticked by at an unusually slow pace for the next few days, with me resenting the fact there were still substantial kilometres standing in the way of seeing him.

Day 190 – 37.6 km
Day 191 – 38.1 km
Day 192 – 34.9 km
Day 193 – 29.5 km

My dad would bus from Winnipeg to Thunder Bay, a ten-hour ride through Kenora and the western edge of the Canadian Shield. My goal was to get as close as possible to Thunder Bay before taking another rest day. I had run east of Nipigon to the northwest shore of Lake Superior, but I was more than 100 kilometres from Canada's gateway to the west. I was beat. *A couple of days off will restore my strength.* As I drove toward Thunder Bay, I smelled something burning. Smoke wafted up from somewhere underneath my driver's seat. I pulled over in an attempt to locate the source but had no luck. Remarkably, my need for a shower and a comfortable bed superseded my fear of the RV bursting into flames. I pushed the hazards button on the dash and slowly made my way into Thunder Bay, this time contemplating my relationship with the RV. *How could this soulless, pulseless, inanimate object have had such control over the past six months?* I knew my dad would have the answer.

CHAPTER 7

Like Father, Like Son

I understood all the clichés attached to journeys. Sometimes the road is straight. Sometimes it's winding. There are ups, downs and often potholes that wreak havoc, even if momentarily. In hindsight, they make good stories. But in the remoteness of Northern Ontario, accepting the hardships and obstacles synonymous with journeys and expeditions was easier said than done. I was committed to this journey and could already sense it was meaningful. But it was fraught with frustration.

Both the obstacle and the cause of frustration on my 7600-kilometre journey was a 1984 Chevrolet Citation. Though it paled in comparison to the impediments others sometimes faced on their journeys – lost limbs, sunken ships and the like – the ramshackle RV nearly completely derailed my plans to move west. Had it not been for Koona, it would have been tempting to ditch the support vehicle altogether, place my essentials in a buggy like Jean Beliveau and continue on unsupported. But having Koona along was non-negotiable – there was no intention of being apart from her for the next three months. So we soldiered on, making the best of the decades-old home on wheels.

After five weeks of wayfinding through Northern Ontario on my own, I now had someone else to help tackle problems and find solutions – someone I valued and trusted more than almost anyone. I picked my dad up from the Greyhound bus station in Thunder Bay and managed to utter only one word before my wall of resolve came tumbling down.

"Father!"

"Son, good to see you," he said as he hugged me.

The word *son* had changed context over the years. As a kid, hearing my dad say the word inferred I had done something wrong. In my teenage years, it was more nuanced: it could mean he wanted to have a heart-to-heart, he was disappointed and about to impart a life lesson or about to say something cheeky: "Son, you don't have a curfew, the car has a curfew." The use of the word was diverse in those formative years, but as I moved away from home – actually my parents moved away from me – and I saw them less and less, the word "son" became a term of endearment from my father. He is one of my best friends, and I am still his son.

We tossed his bags into the Citation and headed to a noisy pizza joint straightaway, where we hunkered down over slices of pepperoni and cheese and explored options to remedy the RV situation. It was tough to greet my dad dejected. I had not seen him since those few days in Toronto, which seemed to exist in a past life. At this stage of the journey I was exhausted, wanting someone else to make the decisions while I ran the kilometres. I knew my father would support me in whatever decisions I made, but that he would stop short of making them for me. Problem solving had been an ongoing part of my journey for more than six months, and he renewed my confidence in my ability to navigate a solution to my RV woes.

The following morning, I was singularly focused on fixing the Citation. By dinnertime, however, I was the new owner of a 1983 Glendale RV, slightly less decrepit than the Citation. In the span of eight hours, we had found Bob, a Thunder Bay local who was selling the Glendale and willing to lower the price in exchange for the Citation. Bob was looking for a trailer to park at his small cabin that would be stationary on his property, providing another bed for visitors. Immobility was an expectation the Citation could fulfill.

Saying goodbye to the Citation was complicated – we had become intertwined in a dysfunctional, codependent relationship. (Well, I'm not so sure it needed me, but I had certainly needed it.) With all of its flaws and misgivings, it had been home for 193 days. But there was no time for sentimentality. If I wanted to make it across the Prairies and over the mountains to the west coast, I needed a reliable support vehicle.

Just as SP's belongings had been emptied out onto a driveway, so too were mine on Bob's driveway. I sorted and transferred everything over to the Glendale, unaware of how much useless junk one can accumulate while trekking across the country. The bathroom of the

Citation was a particular disaster – a dumping ground over the months, collecting nonvital, day-to-day items such as a hand-held vacuum cleaner or apparel I hadn't touched since Newfoundland. Bob was kind enough to not only accept the Citation as is but some of the dirty contents within. The '83 Glendale was a bigger RV at 28 feet; however, the extra room didn't feel like a luxury as much as it was a nuisance for maneuvering. But the price was right and I was desperate. On its inaugural night, we made our home in the parking lot of a Walmart, Dad adjusting to a plywood bed, while I adjusted to my father's snoring.

The next day was tiresome; signing documents, finding banks, adjusting licences, transferring ownership and insurance, getting proper plates – I was bordering on excitement to get back to running. Almost. I was, however, without a doubt, ecstatic to not have to thumb a ride for the next few weeks, and also hopeful having my dad around would alleviate some of the daily stressors, mainly ensuring Koona was all right. As we drove east toward Nipigon, I gave him a crash course on everything support related. He made clear his goal was to be as helpful as possible for the next three weeks, but I was conscious of his dual role: logistician and dad. It was odd giving my dad directions after so many years of the opposite being true. His grace was evident as he listened to me ramble on about the mechanics of the day.

"Son, I think I've got it," he finally chimed in.

That afternoon, the second half of my run was again

plagued with knee pain. My legs riotously protested the return to the demanding highway routine, and I steadily accumulated fewer kilometres with each passing hour. As I crossed the dramatic, cabled Nipigon River Bridge that marked the end of my day, I saw the Glendale parked and my dad standing at the edge of the highway, looking my way. As I got closer and slowed to a walk, I could see tears in his eyes. Being a runner, he knew I'd taken much longer than I should have to complete the day's distance, and he grew anxious waiting, as any parent would. I watched his initial relief become a deepened understanding of the challenge I faced daily. For months, he and my mom were avid followers of my blog posts, they tracked my progress on a wall-sized map and I had chatted with them by phone more than anyone else. My dad arrived believing he understood the daily ins and outs of my newly acquired nomadic life. But on that day he lived it. He felt the hot sun, he saw the tractor-trailers speed past, the easily distracted motorists, my bum knee. His embrace said all of those things.

"I'm so proud of you, son."

🍁

My dad grew up in Hamilton, the oldest of three brothers. He played a lot of sports in his youth, but he excelled at football during high school and university. He got good enough that he played briefly for the farm team of the Hamilton Tiger-Cats, until an injury sidelined him and he was forced to choose another path. He became a runner in his late 20s and, for the past 45 years or so, he has woken up at 4:50 a.m. (one of the few qualities I don't take after), laced up his shoes and gone for a run every day. There have been short periods when injury has sidelined him, or he won't wake up until 6 a.m. to start his day, but now, at age 80, he still enjoys his morning jaunt around Assiniboine Park in Winnipeg.

When I was in Grade 6 and our family lived in Winnipeg, my dad decided to run a half-marathon. He had run one before but was motivated by the long-standing tradition of runners wanting to beat their previous time. As is the case most often, races are held on Sunday mornings – this posed a problem, as his responsibilities within the church were a conflict. Luckily, my mother was a minister as well, so she did the service the Sunday morning of my dad's race. Right before my mother greeted the congregation, she informed me that my dad had finished the marathon but had collapsed of dehydration at the finish line and was rushed to a nearby hospital. He was OK though.

I sat through the first few minutes of the service, unable to sing the selected hymns, my mind racing as the congregation recited the Lord's Prayer. I couldn't bear the thought of my father alone and unwell in a hospital bed. So I snuck out of the pew and sprinted to the hospital nearby. I ran with urgency and determination, believing that every minute counted. Upon arrival, I huffed and puffed at the desk in the emergency department and politely asked for my father's room. "No such name is registered," I was told. I was confused. It took a few minutes for the nurse to discover and inform me he had been taken to another hospital, a hospital not within sprinting distance. I walked back to church – slowly – ensuring my arrival post sermon. After the service, my mom drove my sisters and me to the hospital and I was at his bedside, relieved to see the intravenous fluids were helping and he was alert. At 12, I couldn't perceive the effort and commitment running a half-marathon took, but I knew I was proud of my dad.

Before heading to Newfoundland to begin running across the country, I stayed with my parents in Winnipeg for six weeks. Three adults under one roof for weeks on end had challenges, like my inability to do my dishes right away or to do the laundry piling up in my makeshift bedroom corner. Being under a parent's roof for too long often has a habit of transporting us back to the moody teen years. But we made it through unscathed, minus a few dirty dishes left hidden in the basement. One brisk Saturday morning, my dad waited until I woke at the leisurely hour of 8 a.m. to run with me. Our strides were in sync, and the crunching of snow beneath our feet kept our tempo. We spoke little as we made our way around Assiniboine Park, birch trees naked without their leaves and deer quietly foraging the forest. It's been said by numerous friends that I live in my head, content with my own thoughts and company. I suppose I come by it honestly. The crisp air filled our lungs and the frost nipped our noses. I'll always remember that run. Sometimes it takes the passage of time to provide the necessary clarity – especially where parents and children are concerned. I now more fully understand how my dad played an integral role in my love for the outdoors.

🍁

Attempting to put yourself in someone else's shoes, figuratively speaking, is never easy. On Day 200, I awoke and lay in my upper bunk contemplating Terry Fox. On that day I was to run the last stretch of highway Terry Fox ran before his cancer returned and forced him to stop. Terry Fox lives in our national conscience as a youthful image of quiet determination and unyielding perseverance, and, yet, as I laced up and tried to put myself in his shoes, I wondered: *Did Terry Fox have moments of doubt? Did he question the impact of his actions and whether good would come from them, like I did?*

I wonder if we revere high profile athletes who overcome injuries and believe they are in some way superhuman. If soldiers are brave, cancer patients are warriors and explorers are trailblazers, are our stories somehow lessened if we show vulnerability or doubt? What drives us to put others on pedestals and believe their resolve is somehow greater than our own?

As I approached the turnoff for the Terry Fox monument east of Thunder Bay, I was overwhelmed. The memorial and lookout were created to commemorate the nearby spot where Terry Fox was forced to stop running because of the cancer that had spread from his bones to his lungs on August 31, 1980, when he was 22. I was humbled by his spirit and inspired by his legacy. Although he has become one of the most prominent Canadians and is often called a hero, Terry Fox was a quiet hero. He challenged us to make a difference in our lives – to translate our beliefs into action. Of course, there will be questions along the way, and moments of doubt as well. As we waver on our own path, we can consider his determination and perseverance, even amid the uncertainty. He inspires us to embody the spirit with which he committed to his Marathon of Hope, encouraging us to live out our own convictions. Terry Fox can inspire us to become heroes within the communities we live in.

As I ran up the path to the monument, my eyes filled with tears, a blurry Lake Superior in the distance, glistening from the afternoon sun. This was the moment I had wanted all those months ago on my first day in St. John's when I began this journey. The parking lot was nearly empty on this weekday morning, the statue of Terry Fox sitting quiet and unassuming. After touching the fenced-off enclosure to the monument, I turned to see my dad, who had been waiting for my arrival. If there was anyone I wanted to share this moment with, it was my father. Tears streamed down my face as I hugged him. A family standing nearby watched us, sensing the weight of the moment. My dad stepped toward them and explained the story of my journey to the parents and their daughter as they listened attentively. The little girl stepped toward me and said, "Wow. You really did that?" I nodded my head, unable to say anything.

The Terry Fox monument was also a significant geographic milestone on my cross-country trek; it was a major finish line for me mentally, and it marked the beginning of my run across central Canada. Dad was adapting to the daily routine and my legs were strong – a good combination for moving forward. Not that everything was on the uptick: Dad stripped off the back corner of the RV hitting an unsuspecting boulder while maneuvering at a lunch spot. Also somewhere there was a hole in the new-to-us RV, and mosquitoes were feasting on me, their buzzing an offence to my ears when I needed sleep. The weather in early August was also inconsistent – some days were hot with an unrelenting sun, and others were windy with a cold rain that thrashed me as it raced across the expansive forest and highway.

  Thunder Bay to Shabaqua Corners – 41.3 km
  Shabaqua Corners to Raith – 47 km
  Raith to Upsala – 48.9 km

🍁

Growing up, my parents split domestic duties pretty evenly: Mom did laundry and Dad cleaned the bathrooms. Dad washed the dishes and Mom dried the dishes. Mom was good at delegating too – my sisters and I were proficient in vacuuming, dusting and cleaning our rooms. The one lopsided task was cooking. My mother was the primary cook, which all of my family members would agree was for the best. Although my dad did try. Whether he offered, or whether it was ordered, I'm not sure, but once a week he cooked for the family. In the summertime, his specialty was barbecued hamburgers. In the non-barbequing months, he flip-flopped between two dinners: pancakes or muffins. His chocolate chip banana muffins were a staple for many years in our household. However, the RV did not come equipped with an oven, so I was at the mercy of his limited culinary skills. Thankfully, assembling a sandwich for lunch was fairly straightforward, but I couldn't help but grill my dad daily about our dinner menu, asking sassily what I could look forward to each evening. Admittedly, it didn't really matter – I was ravenous at the end of the day and happily dug into whatever pile of food my dad placed before me, such as beef stir fry with potatoes and corn. As long as I could have two helpings, I was content.

That evening, I finished my run in Upsala, a town north of Lac des Milles Lacs, which was an important fur trade waterway. Dad offered to take me to the restaurant at the Shell station on the highway. As I pushed open the glass door to the diner, wood-panel walls and the hiss of the fryer greeted me. Local patrons and passersby were deeply engrossed in their beige piles of food stacked on their plates. Our fish and chips lived up to most food that is deep-fried, but I suspected my dad was grateful to have the night off from tending to my substantial caloric needs. Later that evening at the campground, we watched as dark clouds moved in behind the small lake where we camped, thunder rumbling in the distance.

Rain and strong northwesterly winds pummelled me the next day. I was grateful to warm up in the support vehicle over lunch and change into dry clothes for the afternoon. By the end of the day, managing 48.3 kilometres into English River felt like a major success. Pork chops, potatoes, corn and broccoli were on the menu, and my dad even managed to find one of our favourite desserts: butter tarts.

Professional athletes and diehard amateurs have long debated the merits of diet, from fine-tuning carb intake or precisely measuring the grams of proteins and fats necessary for peak performance. Fads come and go with seemingly inconclusive results, each study proving the benefit of one dietary component over another: low carb–high fat, high protein–low carb, and now veganism is taking hold.

Admittedly, I had not closely analyzed – or analyzed at all for that matter – the calories that fuelled me daily. I knew I was burning between 3,000 and 5,000 calories most days, but I didn't monitor how I replenished those energy stores. I simply ate to my heart's content. Breakfast was the same almost every morning: toasted bagels lathered in peanut butter, sometimes with a sliced banana on top, finished off by a tall glass of orange juice. Lunches were almost always ham or turkey sandwiches with a side of raw veggies or crackers and hummus, or whatever else I could scrounge from the upper shelves of the RV's food cabinets. Fish, chicken, beef and vegetables were RV dinner staples, with a small portable BBQ that gave each day a casual camping feel. But when restaurants were an option, monochromatic fried food was a delight. And in my family desserts are a must. The sweet tooth I inherited from my father was regularly indulged while running – chocolate was an everyday necessity. I shovelled it in with guiltless pleasure at every break and meal. In the evening, I would snack on chips and salsa, chips and dip, crackers and dip or popcorn. The next day, my body chewed through the calories and dipped into my fat stores. I had lost seven kilograms since Newfoundland and I didn't have an ounce to spare. I am embarrassed to admit my affinity for diet pop during those days. Three cans a day was the norm, and although I knew it wasn't healthy, I succumbed regularly to the fizz and satisfaction of the pseudo-sugary taste. I was absolutely not a role model for fuelling one's body for athletic pursuits – I actually avoided the conversation whenever possible. But as long as my body was replenished each day, I wasn't fussed over what I consumed.

When I had left Thunder Bay, the Manitoba border was in sight – but only figuratively. Literally, it was still more than 500 kilometres and 14 days away. I needed a finish line to look forward to, and Dryden seemed as good an option as any. From English River to Ignace I clocked my farthest one-day distance ever at 56.1 kilometres, a distance I almost matched the next day – the run to Borups Corners was 53.3 kilometres.

There was genuine happiness at the end of each day with the progress I was making, but my ability to converse meaningfully with Dad was often low. I knew these three weeks with him was something that would never happen again, and I was keen on making the most of it. But every evening I felt drained. We talked in short spurts, but the fluidity of longer conversations was lacking. Thankfully, he is content in silence, a blood-related co-conspirator at peace with stillness. He read or relaxed in his lawn chair, letting his thoughts wander under the evening sky.

For ten consecutive days through northwestern Ontario, I averaged 48 kilometres per day. I needed a break and my dad needed to do laundry. He was keen to wash his own clothes, but I imagine the ten days of accumulated sweat that was visible through the salt stains of my crusted T-shirts also needed a scrub. We found a laundromat in Dryden, and while the exhilaration of dropping quarters into washing machine slots was negligible, my legs were thankful for a break. That evening at dinner, I was relaxed and alert enough to converse with my father, although the banter was sporadic and random.

"How has football changed since you used to play?" I asked my dad.

Showboating after a big play or touchdown was at the top of his list.

"What do you look for in a partner?" he asked me.

I went on about the expectations of engagement rings, and how I'd prefer to propose to someone with a canoe rather than an overpriced rock.

"Am I really making a difference doing this, Dad?" I asked.

Like any good parent, he reassured me my convictions mattered. "Yes!" he replied emphatically. "Son, the feedback from students and teachers is proof." He reminded me that it was in fact the summer holidays, and school visits would resume in another month. Our bellies full and sweet tooth indulged, we made our way back to the hotel. He offered a room as a treat for the night, although I suspected he was thankful for a real mattress and a functional bathroom. Koona jumped onto my bed and nestled in beside me. I tried to feign interest in the Blue Jays game my dad turned on, but my eyes quickly grew tired and I drifted off to the sound of baseballs hitting the catcher's mitt.

As I set out the next morning, my legs were energized by the day's break. In less than seven hours, I ran 58.7 kilometres, beating my distance record set earlier that week. The increased distances gave me confidence, and with confidence came determination. If being in the zone could exist while running vast stretches across the country, I was in it. After a night at Bobby's Corner and ten hours of sleep, I left Vermilion Bay eager to have another solid day of running.

Highway 17 was quiet and the surrounding rolling hills left the upcoming landscape to the imagination. I was accustomed to seeing the RV pass by as I ran, in search of a spot to stop at our predetermined distance. But on this morning, with no traffic in sight, the RV slowed in the westbound lane to match my pace and my dad hung his head out of the window, speaking to me across the eastbound lane.

"Son, I'll be OK, but Koona bit me."

"Seriously?" I asked.

"Yes, it's quite deep," he said, showing me his right hand that was wrapped in gauze. "I'm not sure what I did wrong. The people at Bobby's Corner bandaged me up, but I may need to go to the hospital to see if I need stitches."

The highway wasn't the best place to dissect the situation. He assured me again he would be fine and we could chat at my next stop 20 kilometres down the road. My heart sank. Koona was generally a friendly dog, but was prone to crankiness if I tried to take something from her. She was also inconsistent with her tolerance for other people touching her under her neck. My dad had taken Koona for a walk after I left, and back in the RV had placed his hand under her neck to unleash her. She instinctively bit him.

As he drove off, I immediately lost my purpose for the day. I yelled at the sky in frustration and then tears came, and my pace slowed to a barely recognizable jog. I was furious with Koona and sickened she had injured my dad, who was only trying to help. All I could think about were the what-ifs: What if I had told him she didn't need another walk that morning? What if I had told him he needed to swing the leash around to the top of her neck to be undone? Sapped of the will to run, I succumbed to the dreadful monotony of walking.

🍁

Day 213 marked seven months to the day since I had started running from Signal Hill in St. John's. The sky was clear, but as the day progressed a strong headwind pushed my hair up high over my visor, as if I had jammed my fingers into an electrical socket. It was my last day in Ontario – after almost 2500 kilometres in the province, I was about to cross the border into Manitoba. Days earlier, I had surpassed the 5000-kilometre mark of running, and was astounded by the realization that Ontario accounted for half of my entire distance. As I neared the keyhole-shaped sign marking the boundary of the new province, my dad joined me for the last 100 metres in Ontario. His excitement was infectious, and we ran the short distance grinning at each other. He was proud, no doubt, but the border also signalled we were close to his own finish line – his wife and regular day-to-day life waited in Winnipeg. It had been two full weeks since he had taken up my cause and put his life on hold for his son.

We found a campground across the border in Whiteshell Provincial Park and walked over to the Night Hawk Café for a celebratory dinner. The arbitrary line separating the two provinces gave me a tangible sense of hope. It had taken four months, but I could finally tick another province off my list. The weight of the province, over a million square kilometres, was off my back, and as my dad and I enjoyed our burgers and French fries, fatigue was overshadowed by achievement.

My dad left the table, I assumed for a trip to the washroom. I was lost in my deep-fried sustenance when I heard his voice pipe up over the din of the restaurant.

"As you know, one of the responsibilities of parents is to embarrass their children," I heard him say. I looked up and realized he was addressing the other patrons enjoying their dinners.

"I am going to embarrass my son, Colin," he said, pointing my way. "In January, he set out from Signal Hill in Newfoundland to run across Canada. Today, he arrived in the province of Manitoba."

There was spontaneous applause from the approximately 20 people present. He continued, briefly summarizing the goal of Take Me Outside to the interrupted diners. Normally, I would have been mortified by the attention, and embarrassed by my dad's bold display, but, in that moment, I immediately identified with my father's pride and his desire to share it from a genuine place. Later, while we enjoyed a slice of apple pie, a man came over to our table.

"How far do you run each day?" he asked. "How many pairs of running shoes have you been through? How much longer before you finish?" He left offering to pay for our dinner. A woman also approached the table and told her story about crossing on the Newfoundland ferry, a connection to the east coast so many felt. Then two women asked questions about the purpose of the run and slipped $10 into my hands.

"A little something to help."

I grinned at my father once the attention died down.

"Sometimes a dad just has to be a dad," he said.

That evening, we unwrapped his hand and saw how swollen and bruised it was from Koona's bite. It had four distinctive punctures that were quite deep, with shades of purple and black surrounding the swelling. While he didn't require medical attention, I was grateful we were almost to Winnipeg. Dad mapped out the next three days, figuring out where to stop and where to camp for the night. He also convinced me to end at the legislature building in downtown Winnipeg, affectionately called "the ledge," under the watch of the Golden Boy high atop the building's copper dome. I was keen to get the next three days behind me and let my dad worry about the logistics. I had run 14 of the last 15 days and the next three days of running would mean that I'd had one day off in the last 17 days.

The next day, the storied prairie flatness did not disappoint. I left the hills and lakes of the Canadian Shield behind and cruised into the flatlands running from Whiteshell to Prawda. The sky was huge and the roads straight, giving the impression I was quickly cutting a swath through the province. After 51.3 kilometres, and another gas station dinner, I started to anticipate my arrival in the prairie capital.

We were treated to a thunderstorm that night, a common occurrence in a prairie summer as the hot sun cooks off the day's humidity. As I drifted into effortless sleep, I thought about seeing most of my family – my mom, sister and nephew – in the coming days. Gentle raindrops danced on the aluminum roof of the Glendale while thunder again rumbled in the distance.

The next morning, our upcoming arrival in Winnipeg dominated my thoughts. Time with family, the interviews being lined up with morning shows and TV reporters and a long-awaited break from running jockeyed for my attention. From months of precedent, I knew that when my brain checked out, so too did my body; I struggled through the 59.5 kilometres to St. Anne that day.

The next day, refocused, I set out mid-morning, the sun's warmth starting to envelop the landscape. The first 20 kilometres passed as fast as my legs could carry me. When I arrived at the RV for lunch, I could see the city's skyline – my first encounter with the deceiving flatness of the prairies. *It must be close now.* Time slowed and distance stretched as each new kilometre seemed no closer to the tall buildings in the distance than the previous one. Eventually, I closed the gap on the expanse of highway as I approached the east end of the perimeter highway, the ring road encircling Winnipeg. My family had lived in the west end of Winnipeg during my youth and I was frustratingly unfamiliar with the city's eastern perimeter, unsure of my distance to the downtown core and its legislature building.

Finally, I was in the city, running along the sidewalks of St. Boniface, moving slowly past shops and businesses, a welcome distraction from the sluggishness that was setting in. It was only in the last few blocks, as I approached the popular Forks Market at the junction of the Red and Assiniboine rivers, that my bearings returned. Within minutes, I was at the ledge. I could see my mom, my sister Alison and my 3-year-old nephew Dylan cheering in the distance. The Golden Boy, his torch and shaft of wheat symbolizing eternal youth and spirit of enterprise, soared overhead. Relief claimed me as I ran straight into the open arms of my mother. I raised Dylan in my arms toward the sky, making him laugh uncontrollably. The smiles and embrace of family instantly energized me.

CHAPTER 8

Prairie Skies

If I were pressed to call any place home, it would be Winnipeg. I've lived in other places for longer periods, but my connection to the prairie capital runs deep. Maybe it's because my family – my parents and sisters – have chosen to live there and so a familial pull calls me back home. Or perhaps it's the quiet resolve of an underdog. Winnipeg has an undeserved national reputation as the lacklustre, boring city caught between east and west. I recently had a gentleman tell me the best two minutes he spent in Winnipeg were running from one end of the airport to the other for a connecting flight. Even though I can't claim to be from this windy city, I am a champion of Winnipeg and a guardian of its reputation against those who would bully it into something less than it really is.

Stereotypes are limiting, but I've never sensed Winnipegers are trying to prove themselves to the rest of the country. There is a modest confidence in the city, fuelled by a working-class reputation and a discreet understanding that the Winnipeg Jets will indeed win the Stanley Cup one day. On the surface, it can seem like the buildings, the people, the arts and even the sports teams have an impact on how the city defines itself. Just as it's difficult to see below the surface of the muddy waters that give the city its Cree name, so too is it hard to see deep into the heart of Winnipeg. Winnipegers have a resolve, shaped by the city's landscape and weather. The wind roars across the prairies, pushing well below sub-zero temperatures to dangerously cold levels throughout the winter. Years ago, the city recorded seven accumulated weeks of winter at −40°C or colder. Even amid the frigid Winnipeg temperatures, one can consistently find its residents playing shinny on one of the multitude of outdoor community rinks, tobogganing where small hills are found and cross-country skiing down the frozen Assiniboine River. In the summer months, long, hot days are savoured, filled with excursions to "the lake," open-air concerts and festivals.

Louis Riel, considered the founder of Manitoba and a Father of Confederation, has long been regarded as a defender of the Metis people and an advocate of minority rights. Riel lived 41 years before being executed in 1885 by the Canadian government for high treason. His story is remarkably complex and still debated today by scholars, politicians and the general public.

Louis Riel was the eldest of 11 children, whose father became well known in the community, fighting for another Metis fur trader in what became a turning point in the Hudson's Bay Company's monopoly. Riel had a strong sense of who he was from a young age. While the majority of what is written about him focuses on the twists and turns of his political life, little is recorded about his childhood along the eastern bank of the Red River. Buffalo roamed freely in what was then considered the North American prairies; an estimated 50 million bison inhabited the region in the 1800s. The confluence of the Red and the Assiniboine rivers and the surrounding landscape must have contributed to a deep sense of belonging to the Red River Valley where he spent his formative years. Where the Red and Assiniboine rivers converge is now known as "The Forks," but it was a place where First Nations came to meet and trade. It is where the Hudson's Bay Company fought bitterly with the North West Company, and a place where Louis Riel spent the first 14 years of his life. It's a place he would later return to in order to establish a government at the Red River Colony, leading Manitoba to its destiny as Canada's fifth province in 1870.

Much attention is, of course, paid to Riel's tumultuous adult years, but what was his childhood like? Did 5-year-old Louis Riel really differ from a 21st-century equivalent? Those early years of play were certainly spent knee-deep on the Red River's muddy banks: flinging sticks into the murky river and watching the current take them downstream. Or peeling back layers of bark from birch trees and then climbing their branches, testing if they would hold his weight – learning about victory and defeat from nature. Did he run in the tall grass of the flatlands, chasing friends until dusk turned the skies pink and darkness fell? Was it play that fostered learning? Was it play that built character, resilience and confidence? Had young Riel not figured out, or struggled through, the legendary harsh prairie wind and winters, would he have found the resolve to become the leader he did? In *A Fair Country*, John Ralston Saul argues that Canadians, at our core, are a Metis civilization.

> When I dig around in the roots of how we imagine ourselves, how we govern, how we live together in communities – how we treat one another when we are not being stupid – what I find is deeply Aboriginal. Whatever our family tree may look like, our intuitions and common sense as a civilization are more Aboriginal than European or African or Asian, even though we have created elaborate theatrical screens of language, reference and mythology to misrepresent ourselves to ourselves.

Can we therefore surmise that it is our attachment to nature and our land that echoes the sentiment of Indigenous cultures and reverberates through our own? Saul adds, "The Indigenous idea of nature is a philosophy in which humans are a part of nature, not a species chosen to master it." Research is now showing that character traits like resiliency and self-confidence, traits that inspired Riel to lead the Metis people and stand up for equality and inclusion, can be fundamentally linked to our time outside on the land. What then becomes of the 21st-century child, spending their days largely indoors parked in front of a screen an average of more than 40 hours a week? While today's children don't have to endure the harsh, inclement winters that Louis Riel's generation did, have we swung the pendulum too far the other way?

🍁

I relished the time away from the Trans-Canada during my three days off in Winnipeg. It was blissful to be in the home of my parents – deep, restorative sleep came easily in their cool basement. Koona enjoyed the comfort of the dining room at night, the hardwood floors cooler than the carpet downstairs. Perhaps her staying upstairs close to my parents' bedroom was to show my dad some sense of remorse, or so I thought. My parents lived within walking distance of Assiniboine Park, so quiet morning strolls with Koona over the bridge into the serenity of trees, deer and ducks provided a needed break from the east-to-west hum of the highway. My mom and sister had helped line up media interviews around the city, and although I was grateful for the exposure for Take Me Outside, I was more interested in spending time with my family, gathered around the dinner table, talking, laughing and fighting over how many Yorkshire puddings each of us could have.

"Uncle, you only get two!" my nephew Dylan shouted.

"All right, but I guess I'll be getting your dessert then," I retorted, not sure how to one-up a 3-year-old.

In those moments, I wished I lived closer to family. I wanted to be the uncle who took Dylan tobogganing or took my niece, Ceanray, skating at The Forks. The days of Riel's generation, and even my own, of kids running amuck were gone – often replaced with structured activities, organized play dates and a screen-centric existence. The number of devices in a family home has significantly increased from a single, centrally located TV and an Atari 2600 or a Commodore 64. When computers hit the consumer market, they were used primarily for work. During my high school days, my dad's desk sat right outside the door to my basement bedroom, and I could hear the clicking of keys every morning on his Amstrad desktop.

As a teenager, having a computer was low on my list of desires. In fact, I'm not sure it even made the list at all. In the 1960s, well-known Canadian communications theorist Marshall McLuhan predicted our growing obsession with these machines and their potential impact on society when computers were just emerging for use by the general public. McLuhan attended the University of Manitoba and later became an influential philosopher on media discourse. He wrote, "We shape the tools then the tools shape us." These tools – laptops, tablets and smartphones we are attached to much of the day – are shaping our behaviours with unintended consequences, directly impacting our level of human interaction, physical activity and time in nature. The more time we spend inside on these devices, the less time we're spending outside connecting to the land. How will this impact future generations of

Canadians? I wanted Dylan and Ceanray's childhoods to mimic mine, to experience what my generation took for granted: free, unstructured, unsupervised, outdoor play.

🍁

The end of August was quickly approaching and the threat of early snow in the Rockies gave me a sense of urgency. I had 2200 kilometres to go before I reached the west coast, which meant the equivalent of another 52 marathons until my ultimate finish line in Victoria. After an interview with CBC news in front of the legislature building and a quick wardrobe change, I started running. I ran along Portage Avenue, past familiar landmarks, until I arrived at the spot where I had joined the Olympic torchbearer in 1988. The candy store was no longer there and my elementary school, Arthur Oliver, had been turned into a giant grocery store. Cities evolve; businesses change and new buildings replace the old, yet the landscape and familiarity of Portage Avenue remained. As I neared the Perimeter Highway on the city's west end, I was overcome with nostalgia for that day in 1988 when I ran with my friends and the torchbearer in the fleeting glow of childhood. It was that moment, decades ago, when the seed was planted that culminated in my own cross-country run. Grassy fields replaced the mass of concrete on Portage Avenue as I approached the town of Headingley, marking the beginning of the prairies.

🍁

Three weeks into life with the Glendale, RV issues persisted, so my mom offered to help for a few days west of Winnipeg. The tentative arrangement to use their car was solidified when the RV wouldn't start one morning. So, while my dad waited for CAA roadside assistance, my mother bided her time, waiting for me to arrive for lunch west of the city.

It was nice to have my mom's company. I ate my lunch in the passenger seat of their Honda Civic – it was fine for a quick bite, but not the best place to get horizontal to grab a few minutes of shut-eye. Over the course of the morning the wind had picked up, but I was determined to make progress. I gave Mom an approximate distance to my end point and headed back out. The flatness of the afternoon's run was welcome relief, but the push of 65-kilometre-per-hour winds eclipsed the ease of the undemanding landscape. I leaned into the wind, my pace unavoidably slowed. By mid-afternoon, after 38.1 kilometres, I called it a day. For the next few days, I ran west, only to drive back east to sleep in the comfort of my parents' home. The return to RV life loomed. Thankfully, my legs readjusted quickly and my daily distance felt respectable.

Day 221 – 46.1 km
Day 222 – 45.3 km

On Day 223, my mom dropped me at my start point

and later that afternoon my dad drove the RV out to meet us. West of Sidney, I saw its 28-foot frame parked off the Trans-Canada Highway on a secondary road. As I got closer, I could see Mom and Dad sitting in their lawn chairs reading, Koona sprawled in the grass nearby enjoying the shade of a large birch tree. I wished reassuring and encouraging words from parents could be at my disposal every lunch break for the next two months. They had both adjusted their August plans to support me, and as we ate dinner that evening in the Petro-Canada restaurant in Brandon, I tried to block out the fatigue setting in already, and expressed how grateful I was for their help.

"I don't know how to say thanks for all the help you two have given me."

"We're happy to help, Colin," my father replied.

My mom, registering the tiredness in my voice, said, "Colin, you can do this. Look at how far you've come and how many schools you've visited. You're really doing it!"

She wanted desperately for the energy in her voice to shine a light on the doubt and hesitancy residing in the shadows of my mind.

"I know, I know you're right Mom. I just feel like this is never going to end – there is still so much distance to cover."

"One step at a time, son," my dad chimed in, "one day at a time."

My father wasn't prone to uttering clichés, but he

didn't know what else to say. This was something I would have to battle through on my own: indeed *one day at a time.*

The next morning, as I walked Koona around the campground that hugged the Trans-Canada north of Brandon, the reality of being alone again sunk in. Although my legs were strong and I was keen to run, my aversion to hitchhiking was stronger. I had no desire to wait for rides again, wasting precious time to get to the start of the day's run, or to wait with arm extended after five hours of running. After filling my hydration pack with water and snacks, lathering sunscreen on my arms, legs and face, I walked to the east side of the turnoff for Brandon. I passed a young couple who were also looking for a ride and had a dog with them. As I spent the next hour waiting for someone to pick me up, I wondered how long they had waited for rides, how many days they had hitchhiked and what stories they might tell. A half-ton truck eventually picked them up, and I continued to hold my thumb out just a hundred metres away, waiting.

After a luckless hour and a half, defeatism set in. I had stared down long enough to know the placement of each rock and weed sticking out from the ground at my feet. The desire to keep moving west was strong but, on that day, not strong enough. I walked back to the RV, crawled into bed and fell asleep. I woke up crying, a combination of longing for the help of my parents and simply not wanting to run. Actually, it was less about the running and more about the hitchhiking. Five weeks of hitchhiking through Northern Ontario was enough. To face it again for the weeks ahead made me bitter.

In 1987, Marilyn vos Savant, the world's smartest woman by measure of IQ, wrote: "Being defeated is only a temporary condition. Giving up is what makes it permanent." This sentiment perfectly echoed my headspace in the days following my parents' departure. I replaced a day of self-pity and doubt with a renewed sense of determination. I hitched a ride within half an hour, found my starting point and settled into a solid 50-kilometre day.

The next afternoon, I shuttled the RV forward to Virden and parked it beside an A&W. It was late afternoon and I had already run 26 kilometres, but the Saskatchewan border was only another day's run west of Virden if I pushed, so I found myself contemplating a 56-kilometre day. Determined, I walked back to the east end of Virden and again stuck out my thumb. Two young women picked me up in a beat-up Toyota, and after 20 minutes of driving east I started running west. My legs quickly became tired, but I had little choice but to slog through the kilometres back to Virden. My mind went numb. At some point a train passed, catching my attention briefly with its familiar horn. The sun was bright in the prairie sky, but it was lower and the shadows longer than I was accustomed to. My runs typically finished by 6 p.m., but it was 8 p.m. and the sun was slowly dipping toward the horizon.

I would not recommend running along the shoulder of any stretch of the Trans-Canada in the dark, but that evening even the thought of sleepy, disinterested motorists could not deter me from reaching my day's finish line. Moments later, I had a revelation. I remembered passing a small ice cream store on my walk from the RV to the edge of Virden to hitch a ride. My stomach and brain conversed quickly and were in agreement; within seconds I was craving a chocolate milkshake. Actually, craving is an understatement: I needed a chocolate milkshake like I needed my next breath of air. Franchise milkshakes are OK in a pinch, but everything tastes better at an independent ice cream store.

It was 8:10 p.m. How late could the shop be open, even in the height of summer? It had to be open 'til 9 p.m., right? It *had* to be. I checked in on my Garmin GPS watch. I had run 48 kilometres since the girls in the dilapidated Toyota had dropped me off, including my morning distance. I had eight kilometres to go and about 45 minutes before I would lose my chance at a chocolate milkshake. For experienced runners, pounding out eight kilometres in 45 minutes was not necessarily a difficult task. But over the past several months my pace rarely broke 7.5 kilometres in an hour. I was slow, painfully so at times. It was really the only way to run 181 marathons in a nine-month span. But on this warm summer evening, my pace quickened, my determination mounting with each stride.

"Damn it, I am *going* to have a chocolate milkshake tonight!" I yelled at the passing cars.

I found fuel in a seemingly empty tank. I broke into a huge smile when, at the 53-kilometre mark, my pace was that of a 10k race. At 8:55 p.m., I broke stride and calmly walked up to the window of Ice Cream Island without a hint of panic and ordered my shake. As I sat on the picnic table, inhaling what was the best chocolate shake of my life, I was amazed at my determination. My mind – and my stomach – had overcome the utter exhaustion of my body. It was a stark reminder of the power of sheer will. As I tossed out my empty cup, a sign caught my attention – Ice Cream Island was open until 11 p.m. I bellied up to the counter.

"Another chocolate shake, please."

🍁

The elation of crossing over the Saskatchewan border shortly after Virden, thus completing another province, was overshadowed by the desire to book a motel room in Moosomin and enjoy my first shower in nine days.

In Moosomin, I received news that my friend Audrey could drive support for the next few days. This lifted my spirits immediately. I had met Audrey in my graduate studies a few years earlier; she was unequivocally attached to the prairies, having grown up on a farm and now living and teaching in Regina. Audrey also connected me with the Saskatchewan Outdoor and Environmental Education Association (SOEE, now

SaskOutdoors) and, in turn, it lined up a handful of school visits in the coming days, my first since the summer break. Wide-open, ocean-blue skies were a striking backdrop for the golden wheat fields abutting the highway. The expansive scenery provided a boost to my depleted stores of energy.

> Moosomin to Whitewood – 49.8 km
> Whitewood to Grenfell – 49.2 km
> Grenfell to Indian Head – 48.9 km

Approaching the outskirts of Regina as I ran west on the Monday of the September long weekend, I heard the call of a hawk close by. Turning to my right, I was startled to see the hawk swooping directly at me. Before I could question the full extent of what was happening, I dropped to the pavement. The hawk flew right over me, narrowly missing my head. As it gained altitude, I felt sheepish crouched on the side of the highway. I awkwardly straightened myself and glanced at the passing vehicles. I wondered if the dive-bombing bird was an omen but was told later by Audrey it was a typical Regina welcome, raising an eyebrow in her attempt to appease me.

A half hour later, I met up with members of the SOEE Association (now known as SaskOutdoors) who had asked to join me along the Trans-Canada as I entered Regina. I thought I would be joined by fellow runners but instead was surprised by a fleet of bikes. I wondered briefly about the logistics of eight or so bikes joining me on the shoulder of the TCH until I saw another surprise: a police vehicle. As we huddled together, making our way west into Regina, I felt like minor royalty running ahead of the flashing lights. Although the escort felt unnecessarily lavish, it allowed us to swap stories and allowed me to enjoy the cyclists' company without the ever-present concern of speeding vehicles and distracted drivers.

🍁

Growing up, I was always reluctant to go back to school after summer holidays. The freedom of summer vanished as the structure of school returned, and readjusting to school routines was never easy. But after a long summer passed in Northern Ontario and partway across the Prairies, I was glad school was back in session and excited to have students along on my journey again. On the first day back to class, I visited Grant Road Elementary School in Regina. Students sat in the plush grass and reached their hands toward the endless blue sky in response to my questions about their time outside.

"How many of you think spending time outside is important?"

Eighty hands stretched skyward.

"And how does that compare to the amount of time we spend in front of screens?"

I was inspired by the level of engagement from my young audience and hopeful my message would resonate beyond my brief visit.

The uplift from the encounters in Regina was quickly quelled, and Audrey was called back to work. As I ran out of the city, the staggering heat cooked the highway blacktop. I ran in an oven, heat waves radiating off the pavement. After 37 kilometres, I had sucked every last drop of water from the pouch on my back. Empty of water, and with no amenities within a reasonable distance off the highway, I was forced to finish early. The following days were the same – an intense heat beat down on me as I approached Moose Jaw. For four days I was baked by the intense prairie sun. Shade did not seem to exist on the flatlands. But I grew accustomed to my new challenges. I took to pre-planning water sources and also took the time to search for shade for the RV. I was soon back to clocking impressive distances, covering nearly 186 kilometres in three days.

It's tempting to say I was in the heart of Saskatchewan now, but really I was in the heart of the TCH that split the province into north and south. When I crossed gravel or dirt side roads unfurling in either direction, I wondered how long they lasted. How many days could one walk north through farmers' fields before forests started to appear again? The prairie felt endless.

"There is nothing to look at, but everything to look at."

This is how Audrey had described the Prairies to me days earlier. I have an engrained affinity for the plains, having lived in Manitoba and Alberta for part of my childhood. I was more than willing to accept the expertise of a lifelong prairie girl. And, to be fair, her statement holds a lot of truth. I have lost count of the number of people who have mentioned to me the boring drive through Saskatchewan, claiming there is nothing to see but fence posts and endless fields of wheat, canola and barley. Yet there is so much to look at.

Audrey had other commitments, so I was back to hitchhiking. During lunch breaks, I lay in the tall grass, peering into the vast sky and watching trains grow smaller and smaller until I lost them on the distant horizon. "Land of Living Skies" is etched on Saskatchewan licence plates and it's easy to see why: intoxicating sunsets are repeated dusk after dusk and extraordinary cloud formations blossom above. I'm not sure if there are many other places in the world where you can see the amount of sky that hangs over the Canadian Prairies. There is abundant intrigue, found simply by staring upward. Wetlands lined the highway, providing rich and diverse ecosystems, home to a staggering variety of birds. Though waterfowl are likely used to the loud roar of trucks and transports along the highway, they spooked rather easily at a 170-pound runner. I felt bad disrupting the daily routines of the ducks and mallards as they flapped their wings, frantically taking flight to escape the unfamiliar sound of my footsteps. Cows gave me their full attention as well, eyeing me suspiciously as I spoke calmly back to them.

"I'm just another human being – it's all right."

Beautiful wildflowers lined the road, a testament to the splendour that can be found alongside the mundaneness of asphalt and steel. Hawks soared high above looking for their next meal as I examined the ground, attempting to avoid the crunch of grasshoppers, crickets, caterpillars and butterflies underfoot. Adaptation enables grasshoppers to stick their landing when jumping in grass, but if they stay on the pavement, their "hop" often results in a crash landing. They tumbled and rolled in an entertaining fashion that was anything but graceful. If I needed a reminder of the enormity of our country, moving beneath fluctuating skies and fixating on the minutiae underfoot on the Prairies provided it. The vastness of land and sky was impossible to quantify.

What I could quantify was the number of kilometres I was putting in each day. The stretch through the Prairies was, without question, my strongest running to date. I was discouraged with my return to pleading for rides, and although the fatigue of wanting to be done was ever-present, my body felt powerful. The motivation to keep pushing was driven by the distances tallied on my watch.

Day 240 – 55.6 km (arrived in Swift Current)
Day 241 – 47.2 km (chilly start at 0°C)
Day 242 – 49 km (struggled with headwind)
Day 243 – 45.6 km (struggled with headwind)
Day 244 – 40.1 km (struggled with headwind – crossed the Alberta border)
Day 245 – 42.4 km (struggled with headwind)

❦

Crossing the border into Alberta meant the start of my third and last prairie province. I was severely fatigued, but with Calgary in my sights and little more than rolling hills and fields surrounding me, there was no choice but to keep plodding along. I sought refuge in snippets of shade and was surprised by roadside ditches strewn with garbage – Tim Hortons cups all over the place. Throughout the Prairies, items like magazines, toothbrushes and glasses lay dormant along the highway, and I pondered the decision-making process that resulted in someone deciding to eject an item from their vehicle at highway speed. I had also seen numerous plastic bottles that I initially mistook for apple juice. My imagination got away from me on these long days, and I cringed at the thought of men urinating in a plastic bottle tucked in between their legs. The precision needed to perform such a task made me wonder why so many bathroom seats were splattered with such careless abandon. I questioned the mindset one must have to roll down the window, while travelling at 100 km/h, and hurl the warm plastic bottle across the passenger's seat out onto unsuspecting grasshoppers trying to stick their landings on the shoulder. The horror.

After a day of rest and a chance to avoid the sun most of the day in Medicine Hat, I continued chugging westward along wire fences where massive farm equipment toiled in the fields beyond. It was three hours to Calgary by car, but it would take me seven days to run to the Stampede City. I was drained, cranky and sunburnt, yet determined. I had school visits lined up in Calgary and its neighbouring communities and was slightly behind on time. A loose plan had also started to fall into place for my last day, the final finish line at my alma mater, Royal Roads University in Victoria – an eventuality I could not comprehend.

CHAPTER 9

Homestretch

"How do you think you're going to leave your mark?"

This was the question Sarah Ketcheson asked her class of Grade 5 and 6 students after my presentation at Sherwood School in Calgary. "Ms. K.," as the students called her, had taught for years but was new to the school. After hearing from a friend of hers, who was a friend of mine, about someone running across Canada, she reached out to request a school visit. She had been working with her students on the theme of footprints and the metaphorical marks we leave on this planet. Teaching 12-year-olds about convictions was not straightforward, but they more easily grasped the concept of the individual imprints they could both make and leave. And they understood the mark I was trying to leave: put down the screens and get outside.

Ms. K. was one of hundreds of teachers I met across the country, and although each visit was brief, there was a connection I felt with these educators working hard to shape the minds of future generations. She had asked me to visit her school because she believed in the message of Take Me Outside. Although my cross-country run was nearly over – even with hundreds of kilometres to go – her class followed my progress to the west coast and continued talking about footprints. One of her more challenging students, who couldn't sit still in class and was prone to outbursts, was drawn to my journey. I received emails from him over the subsequent weeks and he asked Ms. K. every day where I was running. Ms. K. is the kind of teacher who bends over backwards for her students, guiding their progress and supporting their interests, hoping to maximize her positive impact on their lives in the year they spend together. So many of the teachers I had met were the same: giving, empathetic, committed and nurturing.

In the years to come, I became good friends with Ms. K. – Sarah – finding various outdoor adventures in the mountains with mutual friends who, more often than not, prompted lengthy discussions about education. I saw how she invested in her students, and her commitment to taking students outside to play, to learn and to explore was not just limited to her time at school. She lived what she taught, committing as much time as she could afford to her own outdoor time playing, learning and exploring. She embodied one of my favourite quotes from Parker Palmer: "You teach who you are." Palmer is an American educator, author and activist who focuses on myriad issues within education. In his book *Courage to Teach*, he writes, "Good teaching cannot be reduced to good technique; good teaching comes from the identity and integrity of the teacher." For Sarah, fostering a connection with nature is a commitment she made in both her personal and professional life. Her identity and integrity as a teacher is based on her own connection to the outdoors and the natural environment.

🍁

After several school visits in both Calgary and Red Deer, the mountains were calling. In the weeks leading up to my arrival at the foothills, I began to feel anxious about travelling through the Rockies solo, without someone to drive support. I knew remote stretches lay ahead in the mountains, and the thought of hitchhiking every day for weeks was demoralizing. I had put out some feelers and Jennifer, a colleague from Ontario, agreed to dedicate three weeks of her life to getting me to the coast. Jen had been immersed in outdoor and environmental education for years in Ontario, teaching students about the value and enjoyment of the land we live on. She too embodied her own connection to the land in how she taught students. She would eventually move to Calgary to do a PhD in Indigenous studies at the University of Calgary.

Jen met me at a campground just west of Calgary's Canada Olympic Park, the venue for bobsled, luge, ski jumping and freestyle skiing at the 1988 Winter Olympics. The 90-metre ski jump stood out. Its shape was parallel to the hill it sat on, except for a small portion at the end, which hoists athletes into the air before gracefully rejoining the slope of the earth beneath. I remembered the footage on TV of Eddie the Eagle landing his ski jumps significantly shorter than his competitors, but in spite of this the crowd roaring each time he came to a stop. With the Olympic cauldron located in downtown Calgary, I realized it had held the same flame that had ignited the dream I was currently closing in on. As I gazed out onto the slope and recalled those childhood memories, Jen awaited instructions on what lay ahead. She got a crash course on how to drive a 28-foot RV with a sometimes temperamental husky, coupled with the lowdown on the non-vehicle-related support I hoped for – meal prep, school bookings and any media – to finish off the remaining 1000 kilometres.

"How are you feeling about this now that you're here?" I asked.

"I'm good," was all she said.

I didn't know Jen well, but I knew she believed in what I was doing, and that was enough. We tried to find our groove as we left the foothills and drew closer to the eastern edge of the Rocky Mountains. Jen quickly learned the dance needed to maneuver the confines of the RV, and there was a casual acceptance to the evening routine after the day was done. Jen was an avid reader, and although content with the silence of two people in a confined space, we quickly found ourselves immersed in easy conversations and I felt at ease with the weeks to come.

I could see the snow-tipped peaks rising from the horizon to the west, but it would take two full days to arrive under the massifs. As I inched closer, I could feel the majestic beauty of the mountains. Each time I gained another view of them in the distance, sheer awe evoked a visceral response and goose bumps pimpled my arms. I yelled with child-like excitement at the anticipation of seeing and feeling the limestone and shale formed more than 100 million years ago. I was mesmerized by the height of each mountain, contemplating its treeline and the amount of exposed rock that formed to the summit. Just as well-known constellations catch the eye in the night sky, so too did Canmore's famous Three Sisters mountains. Big Sister, Middle Sister and Little Sister, set in a row behind one another, stood out among the other peaks as I approached the booming mountain town, the relief providing a sense of the size of the mountains and the power of the geological forces that pushed them skyward.

Arriving in Canmore was unexpectedly social, for both Jen and me. Among the impressive peaks of Ha Ling, East End of Rundle, Lady Macdonald and Grotto, we reacquainted ourselves with friends who had recently relocated to the idyllic mountain town. On a day off, I strolled along the clear, blue Bow River, hypnotized by the all-natural beauty that draws people from around the globe. The Bow Valley is a recreational paradise: mountain biking, rock climbing, downhill skiing, Nordic skiing, backcountry skiing, scrambling and hundreds upon hundreds of kilometres of trails to hike and run. Several months after dipping my toes into the Pacific, I would return to this valley, calling Banff home and falling in love with its dirt trails on my daily runs.

For now, the brief reprieve from the road was filled with good food and conversations with friends, old and new. For once, I looked forward to the next stage of my journey; I was eager to run through Banff National Park and past world-famous Lake Louise in the coming days.

❦

Banff National Park is Canada's first and oldest national park, and to simply state its year of establishment, 1885, undermines the complicated and nuanced history of the larger Parks Canada story. While Bill Peyto, a pioneer, mountain man and park warden, is said to have "discovered" the hot springs in Banff and the beginnings of the park, a more unbiased history is finally starting to emerge. The stories now included in the park's history acknowledge that human activity existed 10,000 years earlier along Vermilion Lakes, not too far from the hot springs, and that Indigenous Peoples like the Stoney Nakoda and the Tsuut'ina resided in the area well before European settlers arrived. It was on the oft-referenced date in 1885 that Canadian Prime Minister Sir John A. Macdonald officially declared a small portion of the hot springs around the Cave and Basin in Banff to be set aside as a protected area under the Banff Hot Springs Reserve, which expanded a couple of years later to 674 square kilometres and was named Rocky Mountain Parks. Today, Banff National Park protects 6641 square kilometres within the Rocky Mountains and has been designated a UNESCO World Heritage Site.

Journalist-turned-conservationist J. B. Harkin played an integral role in the establishment of our national parks system, eventually being deemed by many as the "father of Canada's national parks." In E. J. Hart's book *J.B. Harkin*, he explains how Banff National Park expanded and other parks began to emerge. The Canadian public was largely in the dark about new land use, and it was Harkin in his role of commissioner who had to "not only sell the populace on the need for parks but also to convince them to be prepared to fight for their protection." By the mid-1890s, the mindset of Canadians seemed to be shifting, "no longer thinking of nature as simply something that provided endless resources for their personal use. Rather, it had limits and more positive humanizing elements." In 1912, Harkin's first *Report of the Commissioner of Dominion Parks* was submitted and contained a section titled "Advantages of National Parks" arguing the importance of recreational opportunities. Harkin wrote that the parks existed "for the benefit, advantage and enjoyment of the people of Canada." In subsequent reports throughout his years, he focused on the sense of play afforded to Canadians by our parks.

> The play spirit seems to be one of the strongest instincts in the human being…. In the final analysis, people play because of the results that follow, whether the play be in the form of athletics or entertainment or outing, it matters not, they feel they know they have benefitted

> by it, the recreation has been a tonic for them. It therefore seems that play is essential to the well-being of "man"; if he is weakened, play is one of the most important means to effect his restoration.

Today, Canadians recreate in more than 48 national parks and reserves covering more than 340,000 square kilometres from coast to coast to coast.

Parks Canada now engages the Banff region's Indigenous Peoples toward the common goal of land stewardship with the intent of protecting the park's delicate ecosystems. A commonality between a growing number of Indigenous and non-Indigenous Peoples is a desire to care for the land. There are difficult conversations and no easy answers when issues like mineral rights and pipelines surface. We pit one group against another and lose the grey area critical to the conversation – we are prone to black and white, right and wrong. Space for subtleties appears limited as we grapple with arguably our most pressing issue: our impact on the ecosystem and the future of our planet.

🍁

It was hard to leave the beautiful Bow Valley at the end of my three-day break, but the cold mornings of early October had arrived and the larches revealed their golden winter hue. After a day's run in the Lake Louise area, Jen and I took the opportunity to drive up the road and head to Moraine Lake, a glacier-fed lake in the Valley of the Ten Peaks, whose iconic views have captivated photographers from all over the world. Jen and I marvelled at the emerald water and the giant peaks hovering tall above, engulfing the area below and resulting in jaw-dropping awe. Years later, when I lived in Banff, my parents came to visit and we also drove to Moraine Lake. As we walked the trails adjacent to the water, my mom found solitude on a nearby bench and broke into tears. In her childhood, her parents had brought her to Moraine Lake, and memories flooded in, both her parents having passed away. Landscapes have a unique ability to evoke a powerful sense of place.

On Day 261, I left Banff National Park, west of Lake Louise, and after 40.3 kilometres, arrived at the eastern edge of British Columbia. I hadn't smiled so big since I finished Newfoundland and set sail for Nova Scotia more than eight months earlier. It was the only province left between me and the Pacific Ocean. I now knew I would complete what I set out to do. To celebrate entering BC, Jen cooked a chicken curry I inhaled within minutes.

The following day, after 55.2 kilometres of twists and turns, ups and downs, I finished east of Golden. We drove south to Invermere, where I had been invited to speak at the town's schools, as well as at an evening chat with the Columbia Basin Environmental Education Network (CBEEN). CBEEN is a group of educators committed to fostering outdoor learning across the East

Kootenays. The network has done significant work in connecting students to the land but also building bridges with Indigenous communities, incorporating a more traditional way of learning. In the years to follow, CBEEN would become a strong ally and partner with Take Me Outside.

After numerous phone calls and emails, and a realistic tally of the kilometres I needed to run before hitting the west coast, the last day of my journey was set and plans were in place for the finale in Victoria. Renewed focus was imperative in the coming days to climb over the remote stretch at Rogers Pass. Snow was common through the mountains in late September and early October, so making short work of the pass was a necessity. There was also the driving force of completion – my body was tired and my mind weary. With the end in sight, finding the mental stamina to run big distances each day was becoming more and more difficult. I had driven through Rogers Pass numerous times but couldn't comprehend running over those mountains into the clouds and past the Illecillewaet Glacier. The last eight kilometres of Day 264 foreshadowed what was to come; I ended the day's run with a solid ascent toward the pass. The sun was beginning to hide behind the mountains, and the cool air felt good as I slowed to finish parallel to the Columbia River, which would soon empty into Kinbasket Lake before turning south toward the coast.

The next morning, as expected, was a consistent climb. The hard work warmed me after the day's chilly start.

Running through the narrow valley surrounded by the tall peaks of the Selkirk Mountains provided astonishing vistas that would have been enjoyed more if I had the energy to look up.

The Canadian Pacific Railway built tracks through the pass in the 1880s as a means to connect the prairies to the coast. Because of the frequency of avalanches, 31 snowsheds were built over the next several years to enable travel through the winter. However, in early March of 1910, Canada's worst avalanche disaster occurred, killing 62 men who were clearing snow off the tracks. In the late 1950s, the Trans-Canada Highway was built through the pass and several snowsheds were added to avoid avalanche danger. For a couple of the snowsheds, I was able to run on the outside of the concrete tunnel – the southern edge butting up against trees. But there were a couple not accessible on the outside, which meant running through the tunnel. I plastered myself against the raised curb hugging the south wall and tried to make short work of the dimly lit structures. Reaching the summit of the pass felt satisfying, but it was chilly, and I was fearful of snow and the RV getting stuck, or, worse, being turned around and told to wait on the east side. If significant snow came, the pass would be closed due to the possibility of an avalanche. I crossed my fingers in a bid for decent weather.

The following day, I pounded downhill on the approach to Revelstoke. Of course, descending is less strenuous than ascending, but following 50 kilometres of climbing my legs were jelly and I speed-wobbled my way down from the pass. Expansive swaths of forest and rock distracted me as I searched for small waterfalls coming off the mountains.

A few kilometres west of Revelstoke, we found a campground and, after a shorter day of running, Jen insisted on an impromptu Thanksgiving celebration. Her suggestions for our celebration included wearing lumberjack shirts, listening to the Arthur Awards on the *Vinyl Cafe* with Stuart McLean and going for a swim in a nearby lake. We achieved one out of three, listening to CBC Radio while Jen prepared a Thanksgiving meal with the limited kitchen accoutrements in the Glendale. Over potatoes and roast chicken, we shared what we were thankful for.

"Family," Jen said.

"Agreed. And friends," I responded, adding, "Good food too."

"And Stuart McLean," Jen added.

I was also grateful for Canada. Even as we reconcile the sordid history of our country, it's challenging to think of a better place to call home. Travelling across Canada by foot enabled me to gain intimate knowledge of the intricacies of our land and its people, details missed by car or rail or plane travel. For this I was also thankful.

I was swallowed up by incomprehensible beauty during the next three days. At every turn I was greeted with postcard-worthy lakes, forests and mountain vistas. With a timeline now in place, the stress of undertaking bigger daily distances weighed heavily. The unfortunate by-product of this was staring at my shoes while I eked out kilometres, trying to make significant daily progress. Fifty-four kilometres to Sicamous, the houseboating capital of Canada; 52 kilometres to the west side of Salmon Arm; 44 kilometres to the Shuswap. I daydreamed about paddling a canoe in each lake I passed, imagining the paddle carving quietly through the water and spinning off silent whirlpools. Instead, the monotonous metronome of my feet beating along the highway continued.

On the outskirts of Salmon Arm, while watching the asphalt pass underfoot, something unusual caught my eye in the ditch – something other than the weeds, wildflowers and trash that had been a consistent presence. I did a double take, then stopped running and bent down to examine my find. Wet and muddy from the previous days of rain, a purse lay open in the ditch, its contents spilled out onto the grass and dandelions. There was a wallet with identification in it. I found a phone number and called.

"Hi, this is going to sound a bit odd, but I'm running across Canada and I just found your purse in the ditch outside of town," I said, trying to sound casual.

"On my god!" I heard on the other end of the line.

A Salmon Arm resident had her purse stolen from her car the previous week. We met up briefly close to town, and I handed her back her belongings. She was grateful for the return of her wallet and the other contents of the purse. As thanks, she made a small donation to Take Me Outside. It felt good to brighten someone's day.

Just as I had wondered how far I could walk north or south through farmers' fields in Saskatchewan, I similarly wondered how far I could go if I turned north and started walking through the dense forest of British Columbia. What wildlife would I encounter? How long could I sustain myself drinking from the clear, running streams and consuming the abundant edible plants?

As we drove into Kamloops for a school visit at Beattie Elementary, I noticed a sign indicating pedestrians were not allowed on the Trans-Canada Highway. It was a fairly busy section of the thoroughfare, dissecting the city with numerous turnoffs and exits. I planned on running the Coquihalla Highway but was now concerned I might not be allowed to run this section, in which case I would have to backtrack and find an alternative. I had not missed a section of the cross-country traverse in almost nine months, and finding an alternative prevailed over the possibility that I would get kicked off the highway. So, with maps in hand, Jen and I scouted out a small secondary road east of Kamloops that headed southwest, linking up with the 5A and eventually meeting up with the Coquihalla in Merritt. I spent a full day off the beaten path. Fifty-eight kilometres of farmers' fields and rolling topography were peppered with small lakes and ponds. The trees were turning and the falling leaves brightened the black pavement with yellows and oranges.

After rejoining Highway 5 at Merritt, I knew significant hills lay ahead, and the Coquihalla summit was notorious for its temperamental weather – cooler temperatures were guaranteed and snow was common. The forecast looked promising, but the sooner I could descend the south side of the pass into Hope, the better. The summit pass is the divide between the Coquihalla River and the Coldwater River. To most, it's a means to access the coast from BC's interior or vice versa. But running 7.5 kilometres per hour instead of speeding along at 120 kilometres per hour left me vulnerable to bad weather for longer. My slow pace did allow me to absorb the landscape and the immensity of the surrounding forest that fanned out in every direction, though.

The Coquihalla Summit encompasses a recreation area maintained by BC Parks. Numerous trails for hiking, skiing and snowshoeing wind through the mountains and provide the possibility of a wildlife sighting to those who linger at the highway pass. To me, this illustrated a nationwide commitment to connecting Canadians with the land, even if that means simply getting people out of their cars briefly to take in the views and stretch their legs. I enjoyed the views all day, but after running 52 kilometres and feeling the coldness set in, I was happy to make it over the pass without incident.

The following morning, I charted my course downhill, but more importantly, after days of running south, my route turned west, and I was at last pointed in the direction of the Pacific Ocean. By afternoon, I passed the small municipality of Hope. Running through the pinched valley created by the Fraser River and its adjacent towering peaks I felt just that – hope. I was less than a week away from Point B, my final destination – the end of the road.

The Lower Mainland was truly the homestretch – the last 160 kilometres of this nine-month journey and a relatively straight line to Vancouver. The only substantial deviation came west of Chilliwack in the form of an extremely narrow bridge. Running in the eastbound lanes of the Trans-Canada Highway, I stopped to assess the situation. The bridge was only 15 metres long, but the only way across was via a small curb about 20 centimetres wide that separated the railing of the bridge from the speeding traffic. I could try and shimmy sideways on the curb, hoping traffic would move around me into the passing lane, but the constant flow of cars and trucks made it a daring idea. However, it was such a short distance that if there was a small break in traffic, I could dart across in less than five seconds.

I waited, patiently at first, but after ten minutes of fruitlessly scouting for even the smallest of windows, I grew frustrated. There was no end in sight to the constant flow of vehicles to and from the crowded Lower Mainland. After waiting another five minutes without success, I had no choice but to backtrack slightly, head south along the banks of a small canal for a kilometre, cross at a different bridge and then slowly make my way back to the Trans-Canada. On the cusp of completion, this extra distance was infuriating. I ended the day east of Abbotsford, wet from the rain and physically drained from the last seven days of running; I had accumulated 333 kilometres.

The next day, Jen had a flight to catch back to Ontario, so after a short morning of running, we headed into Vancouver and I would backtrack to run to the ferry at Tsawwassen the next day. Jen had donated three weeks of her life to help me; a causal acquaintance yet with shared convictions. She made me laugh, she cooked delicious meals and she even met me at the end of the day a couple times to run the last few kilometres together. She lived through the chaos that existed in the Glendale, and she saw past my shortcomings during the bad days filled with frustration and doubt. I had made a new friend, and I felt unable to adequately express my thanks. I gave her a hug in the parking lot of her hotel and said we'd connect again soon.

🍁

The stench of a recycling facility combined with wafting manure from nearby farms couldn't deter my upbeat mood as I ran toward the Tsawwassen ferry terminal. I couldn't see the ocean, nor could I smell the salty air, but I knew it was close. It was a faux finish – I would have one more day of running after the ferry ride across to Vancouver Island, followed by a quick jaunt to my final destination. The finish line in Victoria would be busy with students, teachers, friends, colleagues, the media and even my parents. But on this day the finish would be quiet and inconsequential. The Pacific Ocean was there; it had waited for me, ceaselessly sloshing against the peninsula and massive ferry terminal at Tsawwassen.

As I started down the peninsula, extending out into the calm waters of the dark ocean, tears streamed down my face. I was overwhelmed with emotion. I couldn't surmount the thoughts racing through my mind. This had all started with a dream that spanned three decades. I had survived nine months, 7600 kilometres and the equivalent of 181 marathons. Actually, it wasn't survival. It was determination, perseverance and a commitment to my convictions. The seed of an idea sown all those years ago on Portage Avenue when I was a boy was on the cusp of being fully realized. I thought of the people who had supported me: the friends and family, teachers and students who had continued pushing me west over 280 days. I slowed my stride to savour the last few minutes. Seagulls chirped above and somewhere below the ocean waves lapped the pier, and my heart soared.

My friend Meredith from Victoria offered to support me in my final 24 hours and was at the terminal waiting with the RV. I hopped in, gave Koona a big hug and then watched as the ferry pulled away from the terminal, leaving the mainland behind. I had one day of running left. Tomorrow, the finish would be about Take Me Outside. For now, I found solitude on the upper deck of the ferry, contemplating the finality of it all, overrun with emotions. I settled in for the two-hour ride to Vancouver Island.

CHAPTER 10

The End and the Beginning

> It's the quality of one's convictions that determine success, not the number of followers.
>
> —Professor Lupin in *Harry Potter and the Deathly Hallows: Part II*

I paused before taking my first steps from Swartz Bay terminal on Vancouver Island on October 25. It was Day 281, the sky was blue and the west coast air was comfortable - a perfect day for running. Seagulls squawked above, circling the ferry looking for scraps. As I looked back to the east, the ocean was calm, tucked in among the small islands with their rocky shorelines. I tried to absorb all that I could from that moment, to etch into my being the small details of what would be the final day of my cross-country run. Similar to how I searched for a sign on the first day of my run all those months ago in Newfoundland, I searched again on that final day for something to qualify the swell of emotion in my chest, constricting my throat, making it difficult to breathe. Alone, I waited for a signal to commemorate the beginning of the end.

Tears welled in my eyes. I gave up on finding an external source of inspiration and instead turned within. In doing so, I was immediately overwhelmed. Memories from the last nine months darted around my head, fragments of moments tumbled through my mind's eye: struggling through the east coast winter with SP, the faces of a thousand students, hitchhiking through Northern Ontario, time with my dad, the wind in the Prairies. I started crying outside the front entrance of the terminal and, not wanting to be seen, I started running. With vision blurred by the tears streaming down my face, I could hardly see ahead of me. I tried desperately to run through the maze of cars and trucks lined up to catch the ferry. Within minutes, I was on Highway 17 bound for my ultimate finish line at Royal Roads University and the edge of the Pacific Ocean. I eased into my slow, methodical pace – I had more than enough time for the last 34 kilometres.

While the anticipation of finishing was exciting, I had flashes of anxiety. *What would I say today? What happens tomorrow? And the next day? Should I only dip my toe into the ocean or do a full-body plunge?* The advantage to a racing mind was the distraction from the actual running. Kilometres passed effortlessly and by the time I was within ten kilometres of my finish line I had two hours until I was due at Royal Roads. I killed some time in View Royal, leaning against a giant rock to eat a sandwich I had packed, and then stopped a little further down the road to take a phone call from my friend Rob, who was calling to congratulate me. I fiddled about, stopping every few minutes to check my watch, unable to keep a steady rhythm. I remembered sitting in a classroom at Royal Roads University two years earlier for my master's program and saying out loud to my classmates I was, in fact, going to run across Canada. It felt terrifying to say something I wasn't sure was entirely true. But these individuals and professors I was sharing this academic journey with had become family as well. These were my people – people I trusted and respected. They had supported me on my path to the start line and many of them would be there at the finish line when I arrived. Monique, one of my classmates, along with Dr. Kool, the head of my program, had helped plan this final day. I was unsure of all the details, but I felt grateful to know familiar faces would be present as I came to the end of this journey.

Finally, I turned on to Sooke Road, the last significant stretch toward my finish line. To any onlooker who saw me running along the sidewalk it would seem as though I was simply out for a lunchtime jog. The wear and tear of my physical body was not evident. My arms and face appeared healthy as the sun had provided me ample vitamin D over the past nine months. My legs were as strong as they would ever be – it would take several more years before starting to see the toll 181 marathons had on my knees, my feet and my joints.

A group of 12-year-old students from Sangster Elementary were waiting for me as I entered the campus of Royal Roads University. The sign at the entrance welcomed me: "Hooray Colin Harris 'Take Me Outside' Completion of Run St. John's – Victoria." I gave all the students high-fives with a huge smile while an organizer indicated I had to wait, as preparations were still being made further down at the water's edge with media, students and others. Students bombarded me with questions.

"How long have you been running?"
"Did you run on the ferry over?"
"What's your dog's name?"
"What's your favourite food?"

I tried my best to find answers, firing back with rapid questions of my own, learning as much as my brain could process from the excited students. I tried to stay present, because this 7600-kilometre journey was almost over. I wanted to savour every moment of these last few minutes, absorbing the fullness of reaching the end and processing a sense of full completion. We finally got the green light to proceed down to the water's edge from the entrance further up the hill where we had been patiently waiting. The kids were amped, and their pent-up energy put them in a full sprint. I had to rein them in.

"Whoa, guys, slow down!" I laughed.

Pulling a hamstring sprinting to the finish line was not how I envisioned concluding the most momentous accomplishment of my life. After begging a couple of times, they settled in to my pace, although their urge to speed up persisted. Eventually, I succumbed to running faster and together we sprinted down the road. I was so focused on talking and laughing with the students that I realized I hadn't looked up. My eyes shifted upward from the students, and the body of water I had dreamed about for months was now mere steps away. I had actually made it to the Pacific Ocean.

Three weeks prior to my arrival in Victoria, I began contacting schools I had visited over the last nine months to see if they would help celebrate the end of my cross-Canada run on October 25. Trying to coordinate the exact timing of my finish across six time zones was unrealistic, so I asked the teachers to simply commit to taking their students outside for one hour on this day: to do activities outside, to go for a run, to take their learning outside. The purpose was not only to help celebrate the end of the run but also to raise awareness about the importance of getting outside during the school day – of extending the classroom beyond four walls and a desk. I called it "Take Me Outside Day." The students from Sangster Elementary pushing my pace in these last couple of hundred metres were part of thousands of students across Canada who joined me outside on that day. Sangster Elementary, down the road from Royal Roads University, was about to pilot a nature kindergarten and the school's administration wanted to introduce their new program at the end of my run. It was the ideal message to drive home the purpose of my efforts and to springboard the launch of Take Me Outside.

As I neared the ocean, the crowd of supporters chanted, "Go, Colin, Go!" and I fought to hold back tears. Onlookers stepped aside and a narrow path took shape through the crowd, funnelling me to the water. The combination of being an introvert and feeling socially overwhelmed led to an anticlimactic dipping of my toes into the chilly water. I couldn't pull the trigger on thrusting my entire body for dramatic effect, but people were still appreciative as the bottom of my running shoes gingerly skimmed the surface, marking the end of the journey. I was ecstatic on the inside but uncomfortable with the attention from everyone, a lot of them strangers who had gathered for the moment. I struggled to deliver the expected appearance and emotions of someone completing a 7600-kilometre cross-country run. People cheered and I did my best to smile. The media in attendance requested photos, so I gathered the students from Sangster Elementary around me to share the spotlight. I know I hugged several friends and colleagues, but I was distracted trying to locate my parents. I saw my mother among the small crowd and made my way toward her. I could see the tears in her eyes.

"We love you Colin. We're so proud of you," she said, hugging me.

"We're proud of you, son," my dad added, as he reached in for his own hug.

After several interviews, dozens of high-fives, hugs and pictures, I snuck away to the RV in a nearby parking lot to see Koona. I hugged her and, scratching the soft fur at the side of her head, I broke into tears.

"We did it buddy," I cried.

My connection with Koona was one of the most important relationships in my life. Unknowingly, she had played a pivotal role as my faithful supporter; she listened as I worked through problems, shared my joys and my disappointments and nuzzled her head into my arms to indicate her unwavering loyalty. The only things she asked for in return were cuddles and belly scratches. Koona licked the salt from my sweaty arms as she had done so many times during the nine months. She had survived this journey as well. I was on to her ambivalent ruse – surely she had a similar sense of accomplishment as the dog whose well-marked territory stretched across the country.

A more formal proceeding had been planned at Hatley Castle, a historic building on the campus of Royal Roads University. Dr. Kool introduced numerous people who spoke more eloquently than myself, including students who again were able to capture the true essence of why I spent nine months running across this country. As I stood listening, my legs unfamiliar with standing still for a prolonged period, my mind continued to race in all directions. But there was a consistent tone within the words I was hearing – students and adults in the room resonated with the message I had attempted to convey as I ran across the rugged landscape of this country.

That evening, I joined my parents for a dinner of

indulgently delicious carbs and decadent dessert, savouring the taste of completion. Then the confusion set in.

"I wonder whether I'll go for a run tomorrow, just for the fun of it?" I asked.

"At least you won't have to worry about telling a driver how far you want to run," my mom replied.

I no longer had to concern myself with logistics. There were no more school appearances to coordinate and the daily menu of bagels and peanut butter would be put on pause. The routine of running 20 to 25 kilometres in the morning and 20 to 25 in the afternoon was done. I smiled at the thought of not having to give myself any more pep talks about "one day at a time" or "one foot in front of the other." It was over.

After dinner, we drove back to the campus at Royal Roads and walked down to the ocean. I took my sandals off, rolled up my jeans and waded into the ocean. Small waves lapped my ankles, the water cool against my sun-drenched calves. Although I had thought tirelessly about a sense of completion for months, it didn't sink in that I was done. Perhaps it was my calm demeanour, or my inability to display too much excitement in front of others, but the evening seemed to pass just as any other. The sun dipped toward the horizon and birds continued scouring the shoreline for their own meal. I tried to come to terms with the kid in Winnipeg who didn't stop running down Portage Avenue with the Olympic torch and the dream that manifested in that moment.

Years had passed as my dream evolved, molded by life's experiences and my convictions. At times it existed only as a fragment of a thought buried in my subconscious, pushed aside only to reappear in a more vivid form.

Yet here I was, standing in the Pacific Ocean, over 7600 kilometres from where I started this run. Somehow, through perseverance and determination, and the consistent words of encouragement from so many people, I had done it. There was no trophy to hoist over my head, but this dream that had lived inside of me for so long was actually complete. I couldn't remember being more proud of myself, even if it was difficult to show as much in front of others. All of the doubt that had resided in my psyche was washed away with the outgoing tide. I felt true contentment, and with that a sense of happiness I don't think I had ever experienced before.

As I continued to wade through the shallow sea water, my physical body was exhausted. I had pushed myself to the finish line and my tank was indeed empty. Although my legs were stronger than they had ever been, I needed rest. My knees, my joints, my feet, my muscles – I was beginning to feel the impact of each kilometre I had accumulated over the past nine months. It was time to rest and recover. Although tired and drained, my spirit was full with a sublime satisfaction for this personal achievement that had ended hours ago. But with it came a deep sense of gratitude for those I had shared this run across the country with.

For 282 days, I had shared this journey with friends

and family, relying daily on their constant encouragement to keep running west. I had shared this journey with strangers who helped deal with our RV, gave donations at the side of the TCH or picked me up through the remote stretches of Northern Ontario. I had shared this journey with hundreds of teachers and thousands of students who welcomed me into their schools and provided opportunities to talk about how fundamental our time outside is as human beings and about how we often need to be reminded to put down our devices and look up.

I had also shared this journey with the landscape across the country. Every day, that relationship grew as I inched 7600 kilometres from east to west. The stormy weather of a Newfoundland winter and the headwinds through the vast Prairies were difficult moments in that relationship, amid many others. But they helped make me stronger, and, in turn, they deepened my attachment to the land. Every day I spent running, I became more connected to the environment around me. I was part of that environment, but more importantly it was part of me. The trees and the birds, the skies and the terrain, the rivers and the lakes that wove their way through the land I was passing on – they had helped shape who I'd become while chasing this dream.

This connection I had with the people I met and the connection to the land I experienced – the two were not separate. That connection is interwoven in the fabric of what this country entails – who we are and how this land shapes us.

Small, smooth pebbles caressed the bottom of my feet as I walked out of the ocean. My emotions tugged me in different directions: I was elated and proud and simultaneously lost and distraught. The abruptness of crossing the finish line was sudden. There was an empty space where my dream used to reside. As much as I had wanted this journey to end, I now, more than ever, wanted it to continue.

🍁

The transition, however, was not easy. For nine months I had a singular purpose: wake up, run and share the message of Take Me Outside. *What's next?* I asked myself. I had no plan.

After five months of aimless uncertainty in Victoria, I packed up my few belongings and headed to the mountains of the Bow Valley to see if I could search the trails and wilderness of Banff National Park for an answer.

My graduate studies in environmental education and communication had been put on hold during my run across the country. I had finished the course work and started the research for my thesis but had yet to write a word. A nine-month, coast-to-coast journey seemed like justified procrastination, but it wasn't until several months after I had smelled the salty west coast air that I finally sat down in earnest with my research, notes and interviews. My thesis focused on the role of storytellers – particularly storytellers at the Canadian Broadcasting Corporation. As a public broadcaster, CBC regularly covered stories about environmental issues and climate change. I wondered how those stories affected the broadcasters who told them. Did the act of telling those stories shape their environmental world view? Taking the it-never-hurts-to-ask approach, I found myself sitting across from storytellers I had listened to for years: Peter Mansbridge, Judy Maddren, Diana Swain, Paul Kennedy and Bob McDonald from *Quirks & Quarks*. They each had their own take on the role of story and how it impacted them as storytellers.

Stories are ubiquitous; we watch them in movies and read them in books and newspapers. We listen to stories on podcasts or the radio, scroll through them online, exchange them sitting around the dinner table with family or overhear them eavesdropping on a stranger on the bus. Storytelling defines us as a human species. As Karen Blixen, a Danish author who used the pen name Isak Dinesen, said, "To be a person is to have a story to tell." We live. We die. All that's left are our stories. As language was developed, and as it continues to evolve, stories have given us history, culture and identity. Stories are found everywhere, in every culture around the world.

Exploring a literature review for my thesis, I came upon Walter Fisher, who was a professor at the Annenberg School for Communication and Journalism at the University of Southern California. In the 1980s, Fisher did extensive research on stories, developing a communication theory he called the narrative paradigm. In this narrative paradigm, he argues, anyone who listens to a story can pick out the "good parts" and use those parts as a basis for decisions within their lives. He goes on to say, "the ground for determining meaning, validity, rationality and truth must be a narrative context."

When I've had the opportunity to present to high school students and conference attendees over the last several years, I've been drawn to speaking about the importance of telling meaningful stories. *Schindler's List* is a more meaningful story than *Hot Tub Time Machine*. The quest to stop human trafficking is a more meaningful story than the latest Hollywood gossip. In terms of shaping our country's history, I believe Terry Fox's story is arguably more important than Justin Bieber's. It's not to say that there isn't a time and place for more inconsequential stories – often we are drawn to them for entertainment, fun and laughter. But if stories shape our history and culture, then don't we have a responsibility to ensure meaningful stories are being told? Fisher seems to agree. "Obviously, some stories are better than others, more coherent, more *true* to the way people and the world are – in fact and in value." Our stories can't simply be told; they have to be lived with conviction, if, in fact, we want to leave our mark – our "footprint" as Ms. K. shared with her students.

As I reflect on my run across the country and the work of Take Me Outside, while grasping what it means to be a Canadian, there are three things – stories if you will – that have become important to me. These are not only stories to tell but also stories to live. They have sat with me, have shaped me and have further carved my convictions.

The first story is one that revolves around our affinity with screens. In this digital age, it has become a significant story.

Recently, an old friend of mine posted an image on Facebook that triggered a flurry of comments and criticism. The photo showed four dads sitting on the sidelines at the YMCA as their kids participated in an evening activity. Their faces were blurred to protect their identity. All four dads had their heads down, staring at their phones. My friend asked in his post, "Yikes, is this what parenting looks like now?" A swift wave of criticism ensued: "Passing judgment on people when we have no idea what their lives are like seems just as ridiculous, if not more so…" and, "Try not to judge. It's a moment in time they are stealing for themselves. Parenting is 24/7 365 days a year for all your days."

Unfortunately, it seems to me this scenario is becoming anything but a moment. It's impossible to visit a restaurant without seeing family members, friends or even couples on their phones. At work, walking down the street, in bathrooms, in grocery lines, at concerts – people are buried in their phones. I've been to numerous conferences over the past several years dedicated to addressing the shrinking amount of time kids spend in nature versus on screen. At all of these conferences, prominent speakers gave thoughtful keynote addresses, during which dozens of attendees had their heads down in their phones. It's difficult to find public spaces that aren't filled with people staring at their phones, let alone in our own homes, which seem to be sanctuaries for constant screen time. This is not just a parenting issue – my friend's post would more aptly read: "Yikes, is this what being a human looks like now?"

We have indisputable evidence that too much time with our devices has become not only a barrier to the amount of time we spend outside but also a barrier to our creativity, our conversations and to the very way we interact with one another. Screen time not only affects our physical health but our mental, emotional and spiritual health as well. Undeniably, we live in a digital age. Our attachment to devices increasingly stands in the way of face-to-face social interaction and interaction with our natural environment. If we care about the healthy social development of our nation's children, we must take every opportunity we have to model to our younger generations. We will never succeed at this unless we are honest with ourselves about our individual screen-time habits.

This is not a conversation pitting technology against time outside. There is a time and a place for emails, Netflix, texting, catching up on social media; however, currently, the scales appear to be tipped in favour of the digital world. Canadian Malcolm Gladwell, author of bestsellers such as *Blink* and *Outliers*, and known for his social commentary, calls this issue "one of the most troubling phenomena of modern times." Adam Alter's book *Irresistible* gives a stark view of what our future with phones looks like, citing a global study with more than 200,000 participants to examine society's relationship with smartphones. It found 41 per cent of participants had what would be deemed a behavioural addiction to their phone. Another study in 2015 found more than 250 million people around the world have a behavioural addiction to their phone. If you think you're exempt, most devices now track how much time you spend on your phone. The average user is on their device three to four hours daily. Over the course of an adult life, this equates to 11 years spent staring at a phone. And research shows the vast majority of it is logged on social media, scrolling endlessly through Instagram, Twitter, Snapchat, TikTok or Facebook, resulting in increased rates of depression, loneliness, anxiety, sleep deprivation and suicide risk.

Today's kids will never know a world without the technology that has come to pervade most aspects of our lives. Who is taking responsibility to make sure they learn the value and joy and meaning in a life lived outside of our devices in the natural world? Who is their role model for what life looks like without a phone in their hands? In today's age, it's a tough task to even suggest this, as not having our phone within reach is almost unimaginable. But a true role model must venture above and beyond the baseline expectation. As the

American author James Baldwin says, "Children have never been very good at listening to their elders, but they have never failed to imitate them."

If we want the story of our Canadian identity to persist, we must lead the younger generations by example and live this story. This means finding a balance between time spent in the virtual world and time in our wild spaces; otherwise this pillar of the Canadian identity will disappear.

The second story that has become important to me and is the primary focus of Take Me Outside, aside from the concern with the amount of time kids are spending plugged in, is a nationwide effort to encourage and assist educators in the use of nature as a classroom. For Take Me Outside, the idea grew from a single event at Queen's University in 2008. One sunny afternoon, a group of students studying for their undergrads in education were outside partaking in an activity when they saw a couple of kids walk by on the streets of Kingston. One of the students, Ian, yelled to them, "Ask your teacher to take you outside!" The comment had little relevant context – the kids were simply outside enjoying the day. He got his desired response of class clown, a laugh from his classmates. And that was the end of it, or so he thought. But in the coming days, the students in the program kept coming back to those words – they had shared an aha moment. As part of their bachelor of education program, there was an emphasis on outdoor and environmental education. Ian's moment of trying to be funny was, in fact, the essence of what they had been discussing in class all year – students needed to learn outside. As part of their graduation, Laurel Finney, another of the program's students, made T-shirts for her cohort: a couple of trees with the phrase, "Ask your teacher to take you outside" stenciled above them. A movement was born.

My memories of school are selective, but in a general sense I can remember playing outside during recess and at lunchtime. Yet I can't recall ever having class in any of the core subjects outside. Even through junior high and high school the vast majority of my memories entail sitting at a desk in a classroom made of concrete blocks with a tile floor. The closest we got to outside – save the occasional field trip to a farm or zoo – was a lonely window or two, its shaft of natural light dulled by the glare of fluorescent bulbs. Informed by research, that story is changing.

Many of the schools I visited across Canada were building, adopting and creating spaces to be used as outdoor classrooms. Some of these outdoor learning environments were simply a stretch of grass with a smattering of boulders for kids to sit on, or shelters for students to congregate under that provide protection from the elements. Teachers are witnessing the power of outdoor learning – that a land-based and outdoor-focused, experiential, hands-on approach has merits beyond the traditional classroom, be it better problem-solving skills, increased self-confidence or less bullying.

The education system forged ahead with technology in the classroom without blinking an eye. Will the extensive research showing the benefits of outdoor learning gain a foothold in our tech-driven education system?

A friend of Laurel's in that bachelor of education class at Queen's gave me one of those T-shirts, even though I wasn't part of their program. The more I wore it, the more comments I got from strangers – cashiers, servers and other teachers as well. The phrase is a call to action, and regardless of whether people were entrenched in the education system or not, the shirt's caption evoked a response, and often a short conversation. In time, Laurel gracefully granted permission to Take Me Outside to use the shirt's messaging with a new, original design. In the past decade, that shirt has made its way into thousands of homes, thanks in part to sales at MEC stores across the country. The shirt's message advocates for what a growing number of educators already know: learning can indeed happen outdoors.

The third story is a complicated story indeed. It has gripped me for years and continues to impact my daily life. When I was young, in my teens and 20s, the idea of being Canadian seemed pretty straightforward. I was blind to the injustices that plague this country's history. I was blind to the privilege I experienced as a white male and I was blind to the notion that not everyone who lives in Canada identifies with being a Canadian. Sometimes it is hard to come to terms with our identity as a nation. Charlotte Gray explored this in her book,

The Promise of Canada, published for the sesquicentennial celebration in 2017. She concluded, "This country defies definition. There is no master narrative for Canadian history: there are too many stories to package into a tidy, tightly scripted identity."

While I understand Gray's sentiment, and agree there may not be a *master* narrative, I do believe there is a common story that comes the closest. Throughout not only the documented history of this country, but the thousands of years before recorded history, our physical land is the common narrative, bearing witness to the Canadian story. To live on this land is to be shaped by it – the two are inextricably intertwined. Gray argues this in her chapter about Emily Carr, the famous western Canadian artist.

> Of all the artists who made the wilderness a powerful element in the Canadian identity, I view Carr as the most important: she acknowledged that the landscape was peopled and alive before Europeans arrived, not vast and empty as most settlers like to pretend. She was the first to try to capture the spirit of Canada in a modernist style. Her formidable canvases of skies, forest, and First Nations carvings are not macho records of discovery and conquest, but haunting and occasionally erotic paintings of mystery. Her perceptions and images have slowly seeped into the national memory bank.

Gray goes on to contend that Emily Carr continues to tell Canadians about ourselves outside of "the awesome magnificence of Canadian space." She gave our country an identity, not just of the land itself but the people living on it. And while there are many individuals who have contributed in some way to defining our identity, it is "a race without a finish line," says Gray. "Because as the country evolves, so does our collective sense of self."

The story of our nation is a patchwork of individual identities assembled from Indigenous Peoples, European settlers, migrants and refugees. Their stories are the building blocks of Canada. However, the essence that weaves through the fabric of identities is drawn from our rugged coastlines, open tundra and Canadian Shield, the boreal forest with its thin and towering pines, the tall, golden grasses and vast, blue skies of the Prairies and the Rocky Mountain peaks of grandeur. Without these physical spaces, our definition of *Canadian* would be altered. Our land is the common tie that binds us together as Canadians. National unity must rally around not ownership of this land but the privilege of being its stewards.

Driving through stretches of Canada over the last decade, I find little sections of the Trans-Canada will trigger a memory and bring me back to that exact moment during my cross-country journey: a lunch break, a spot where someone stopped to say hi or a pause to marvel at the view around me.

When I tie my laces up and head out the door, I carry

those stories with me. As I run past the jagged bark of pine trees and my feet kick up dirt from the trail, I wonder how I can tell these stories more meaningfully. I ask myself about how I can live these stories more fully. On this path, the trail never ends. It is an endless journey, but one I'm compelled to run on.

EPILOGUE

When it comes to making life decisions, choosing a path or course of action is rarely simple. More often than not, it's complex, with a mixture of terror and exhilaration thrown in. Often, we think there is a right way or a wrong way in choosing these paths, a good decision or a bad one. We're overwhelmed with the weight of a decision and freeze, becoming paralyzed with indecision, unable to weather the storm within. Uncertainty, fear of failure and self-doubt are all barriers that can get in the way of even choosing a path. We sometimes forget the important part is simply starting to run. The direction has bearing, yes, but we don't realize or acknowledge that the path we might choose could lead to great outcomes. The direction of that path may also have multiple wrong ways, but we don't know until we start running, until we start putting one foot in front of the other and actually start down that course. Most times, we can sense whether it's the right path and the right choice – we can feel it in the pit of our stomach. So too can we sense if we're not moving in the right direction. In the end, though, only one thing is required: we just need to start running.

A few days after finishing the run in Victoria, I drove

the RV to Tofino, a few hours north of Victoria along the west coast. I walked Koona leisurely along Long Beach, watching the waves grow with winter approaching. Self-doubt crept in as I thought about what was next for me and for Take Me Outside. But I remembered how much doubt I had before driving east to meet SP and head to Newfoundland to start this dream. Others had doubts as well, some quiet, some vocal. Maybe I should build the organization before embarking on this journey, I was told. Maybe I should wait another year until more pieces like funding and driver support were in place. In fact, maybe I should wait until I had a decent RV. There will always be doubt, whether from others or from within. But, at some point, I had to decide to start running.

Months after finishing, I received a letter indicating I had won an award from the Canadian Network of Environmental Education and Communication for best individual nonprofit organization. I attended the conference in Waterloo to accept the award, and to start building relationships and a network that could help assist the work of Take Me Outside. I had no idea what I was doing or how to run a nonprofit. I questioned myself daily, often paralyzed with my inability to make a decision or head in a certain direction. Sometimes stuck for months on end, I would retreat into a world of doubt. In time, I would come back to what started it all: taking a step forward and starting to run.

A decade later, I'm continuing to run while still trying to figure it out. The organization has grown by working collaboratively with other organizations, school boards and individuals to encourage children and youth to spend more time outside through various projects and initiatives. Since that inaugural day on the last day of my run, our cornerstone initiative, Take Me Outside Day, has seen more than a million students in Canada participate in heading outside to increase awareness about the importance of outdoor learning and spending time outside. Every fall, we hold a student video contest in partnership with the Banff Centre Mountain Film & Book Festival and MEC, asking students across the country to make short videos about why we have the best backyard in the world and why they like spending time in it. We facilitate a year-round outdoor learning challenge where teachers across the country have committed to taking their students outside once a week for the entire school year. We host a winter initiative, encouraging teachers across the country to take their students outside for learning in the heart of a Canadian winter too. We even sell T-shirts that are a call to action and promote Take Me Outside.

We've recently expanded our board of directors and have found funding for a part-time staff member. While I haven't felt a sense of arrival, I know we're running in the right direction. I know this because Take Me Outside is committed to raising awareness and facilitating action on nature connection and outdoor learning in schools across Canada. We believe in a future where spending time outside learning, exploring and playing is a regular and significant part of every student's day. Running a nonprofit is tough: grants come and go, funding is volatile with changes in government and appetites for projects and programs can shift quickly like a change in the wind. All while I continue to work my full-time municipal job in Banff.

When I submitted this manuscript to Rocky Mountain Books in early spring 2020, COVID-19 was only starting to take a firm grip in this country. Six months later, as I wade through edits and revisions in October, the pandemic has a continued presence. The world has been forced to shift in many respects, and our education system has been front and centre as part of that conversation over the last several months. To simply state that outdoor learning needs to be implemented undermines the complexity of the education system – a system and institution where change is slow, arduous and full of barriers. And yet this is a path or course of action that has significant implications for future generations. Dr. Judith Lipp and I wrote an organizational statement below about the potential for outdoor learning within a COVID-19 context, and the possibility that exists for outdoor learning to grow and thrive beyond this pandemic. It was our small way of taking a step forward and trying to contribute to a greater conversation needed within education.

> Outdoor learning needs to become a central feature of the Canadian education system.

Implementation of outdoor learning would have a resounding positive impact on health and wellness, while addressing the immediate health concerns posed by COVID-19. Mental health, obesity, loneliness, screen addiction, climate emergency, and biodiversity collapse, to name a few crises, have now been amplified by the Coronavirus. Consistent and regular outdoor learning offers the perfect remedy to many of these issues and is an evidence-based solution to improving student focus and academic achievement.

Gathering in outdoor spaces has been identified as an important infection control strategy. However, most back to school plans do not include outdoor learning as a core concept and educators are not receiving support or directives to take their classroom outdoors.

The implementation of an outdoor-centred approach may appear daunting in contrast to our current desk-based model, but the arguments for prioritizing outdoor learning are compelling. The benefits of implementing outdoor learning nationally will positively impact individuals, society, and the environment.

Outdoor learning in schools also fosters greater equality in our communities. Public outdoor spaces are not necessarily available in all neighbourhoods, which means some young people can reap the benefits of outdoor time in nature while others cannot. Offering significant, frequent outdoor time at schools can help to address that inequity.

Spending regular time outdoors – simply being in nature or playing and learning near nature – is essential for healthy social, emotional, and physical childhood development. It has also been shown to lead to greater focus, higher cognitive function, and better learning outcomes across the board.

Regular outdoor time also increases physical activity and increases one's confidence with outdoor activities, leading to a more active lifestyle in later years. It boosts mental health, lowers stress, boosts immunity, and connects us to the places we live and the environments we need to protect. Health experts also say it decreases the risk of COVID-19 infection compared to spending time in indoor environments, as confined spaces create greater exposure risk. Physical distancing is simply much easier outside of four walls.

Implementation will require careful consideration and training, but there is a wealth of experience and knowledge in most educational communities. Many schools already have robust outdoor learning departments in place. Further, many educational organizations exist to fill any gaps by offering their expertise in outdoor learning where school staff may need extra support.

This is the time to implement new ways of teaching and learning to better serve our children, our communities, and the wider world. This is an opportunity to not only reduce the spread of Coronavirus but also to address the biggest health, wellness, inequality, and environmental crises of our time. By physically distancing students from four walls and a desk, we can offer our children and youth a liveable future.

Throughout all of this, there is a belief that convictions matter. And I have learned I'm not alone in my convictions. There are thousands of individuals and hundreds of organizations across this country that care deeply about getting young Canadians outside, getting them active and connecting them to the land. The path is becoming well established and we're all running together.

ACKNOWLEDGEMENTS

Since this cross-country journey in 2011, Take Me Outside has developed a network of supporters across the country who have committed to getting more Canadians, particularly younger ones, outside. I am especially grateful to all the educators I have met over the years who are helping shape future generations by connecting them to this land we're so fortunate to live on. Thank you for the work you do.

Taking the first step of running across this country would not have been possible without SP. She not only believed in this journey from the moment I asked her, she committed to it. Through good times and harder ones, I am indebted to her.

To Jennifer MacDonald, who helped me through the Rockies and to the coast. She has always supported this work and is creating a meaningful story of her own through her doctoral studies. There were also numerous friends who helped shuttle me around to various running spots along the Trans-Canada, thank you.

Ray and Cathie Harris, my parents, were instrumental in both their support over the nine-month journey and the process of writing. I will cherish the three weeks I spent with my father in Northern Ontario and Manitoba and can't imagine what this writing process would have looked like without the countless hours when they listened and provided feedback. They have always been my biggest supporters.

My editor, Erin Cipollone, brought a keen eye to this story and a deep understanding for what I was trying to accomplish in telling it.

To Don Gorman and Rocky Mountain Books for your excitement and willingness to bring this story to fruition.

Having the right space to toil about with these words was paramount. Thanks to the Banff Centre library staff for making me feel welcome, and the quiet words of encouragement along the way.

To Geoff Moulton, who read early drafts and helped guide my thoughts.

Thanks to my extended family of my master's program. In myriad ways, you supported me and pushed me to the start line. Monique Booth planned a special last day of arrival, and I'm grateful to others who were able to greet me at the finish line. Dr. Rick Kool – you helped create a special "coheart."

To all the friends, new and old, who stopped on the side of the Trans-Canada to say hi, to run with me, to lend an encouraging word.

To my sisters, Kristen and Alison, for your ongoing support in life, your listening ears and your patience, thank you. To my niece Ceanray and my nephew Dylan,

I am grateful to be your uncle and inspired by the individuals you both are already.

To my main running buddies Shawn Carr, Chris Hughes and Larry Bradley. It seems the best conversations are those out on the trails.

The list of individuals and organizations that have helped mentor, guide and support both Take Me Outside as an organization and myself is too long, although I will single out Judith Lipp and the privilege I've had to work with her the last couple of years as we have tried to build capacity for the organization. I am thankful for everyone I have met over the past decade and am excited to continue to nurture and grow these relationships in the years to come with a common goal of getting more Canadian students outside and connected to the land.

Friends and family are aware of the connection I had with Koona, so I would be remiss not to mention her in this list of thank yous. She was truly a best friend, and I can't imagine this journey of life without her. Her last few years in Banff included walks along the Bow River, burying her head in deep snow and still being fiercely independent.

The final thank you is for Corrie DiManno, who has had to endure my rambling thoughts more than anyone else. She has worn many hats over the last several years: listener, supporter, teammate, partner, cheerleader, editor, best friend and comic relief. She assures me I'm a dream when I'm not a nightmare. Regardless of the path this journey takes us on, I will forever cherish this deep friendship and understanding for one another.

For this story, I have explored the depths of my memory and I take full responsibility for the blueprint I have shared, acknowledging that others have their own stories to tell.

SELECTED SOURCES

Alter, Adam. *Irresistible: The Rise of Addictive Technology and the Business of Keeping Us Hooked*. New York: Penguin Press, 2017.

Carson, Rachel. *Silent Spring*. Boston: Houghton Mifflin, 2002.

Dillard, Annie. *The Writing Life*. New York: Harper & Row, 1989.

Fisher, Walter R. *Human Communication as Narration: Towards a Philosophy of Reason, Value and Action*. Los Angeles, CA: University of Southern California Press, 1989.

Gladwell, Malcolm. *Blink: The Power of Thinking without Thinking*. New York: Little, Brown and Company, 2005.

———. *Outliers: The Story of Success*. New York: Little, Brown and Company, 2008.

Gray, Charlotte. *The Promise of Canada: 150 Years – People and Ideas That Have Shaped Our Country*. Toronto: Simon & Schuster Canada, 2016.

Harris, Kate. *Lands of Lost Borders: Out of Bounds on the Silk Road*. Toronto: Alfred A. Knopf Canada, 2018.

Hart, E. J. *J. B. Harkin: Father of Canada's National Parks*. Edmonton: University of Alberta Press, 2010.

King, Thomas. *The Inconvenient Indian: A Curious Account of Native People in North America*. Toronto: Anchor Canada, 2013.

Kirk, Liz. "The Value of Outdoor Education." *The Star*, July 15, 2019. https://www.thestar.com/opinion/contributors/2019/07/15/the-value-of-outdoor-education.html.

Kula, Irwin. *Yearnings: Ancient Wisdom for Daily Life*. New York: Hyperion, 2006.

McDougall, Christopher. *Born to Run: A Hidden Tribe, Superathletes, and the Greatest Race the World Has Never Seen*. New York: Alfred A. Knopf, 2009.

Northern Ontario Travel: The Official Magazine. https://www.northernontario.travel/group-of-seven/the-group-of-seven-on-lake-superior-s-north-shore?s=1320.

Palmer, Parker. *Courage to Teach: Exploring the Inner Landscape of a Teacher's Life*. San Francisco: Jossey-Bass, 2007.

ParticipACTION. *Pulse Report*. https://www.participaction.com/en-ca/resources/pulse-report.

Robinson, Ken. "Do Schools Kill Creativity? TED2006. https://www.ted.com/talks/sir_ken_robinson_do_schools_kill_creativity?language=en.

Rowling, J. K. *Harry Potter and the Deathly Hollows*. London: Bloomsbury Press, 2014.

Saul, John Ralston. *A Fair Country: Telling Truths about Canada*. Toronto: Viking, 2008.

ABOUT THE AUTHOR

Colin Harris is the founder and executive director of Take Me Outside. He initiated the organization by running 7600 kilometres across Canada over nine months, going into 80 schools across the country and engaging 20,000 students in a conversation about their time spent in front of screens compared to their time spent outside, being active and connecting to nature. Colin has been immersed in the field of outdoor and environmental education for over 15 years. He has been the director of outdoor education at an Ontario-based centre, he has instructed canoe trips for Outward Bound Canada and has worked with Indigenous students in the Western Arctic Leadership Program in the Northwest Territories. He has completed a master's degree in environmental education and communication. He currently lives in Banff, Alberta, and enjoys trail running, writing and continuing to find ways to engage Canadian students in exploring this country's incredible landscapes.

All rights reserved. No part of this publication may be reproduced, stored in a retrieval system, or transmitted in any form or by any means – electronic, mechanical, audio recording, or otherwise – without the written permission of the publisher or a photocopying licence from Access Copyright. Permissions and licensing contribute to a secure and vibrant book industry by helping to support writers and publishers through the purchase of authorized editions and excerpts. To obtain an official licence, please visit accesscopyright.ca or call 1-800-893-5777.